ARTHUR MILLER

After the Fall

with commentary and notes by
BRENDA MURPHY

Series Editor: Enoch Brater

METHUEN DRAMA

Methuen Drama Student Edition

10 9 8 7 6 5 4 3 2 1

This edition first published in the United Kingdom in 2011 by
Methuen Drama
A & C Black Publishers Limited
36 Soho Square
London W1D 3QY
www.methuendrama.com

Copyright © 1964 by Arthur Miller
Subsequently © 2007 The Arthur Miller 2004 Literary and Dramatic Property Trust

Commentary and notes copyright © 2011 by Methuen Drama

The rights of the authors to be identified as the authors of these works have been
asserted by them in accordance with the Copyright, Designs and Patents Act, 1988

Chronology of Arthur Miller by Enoch Brater, with grateful thanks to the Arthur Miller
Society for permission to draw on their 'Brief Chronology of Arthur Miller's Life and
Works'

A CIP catalogue record for this book is available from the British Library

ISBN 978 1 408 12312 6

Commentary and notes typeset by SX Composing DTP, Rayleigh, Essex
Playtext typeset by Country Setting, Kingsdown, Kent
Printed and bound in Great Britain by
CPI Cox & Wyman Ltd, Reading, Berkshire

Contents

Arthur Miller: 1915–2005

1915   17 October: Arthur Asher Miller born in New York City, the second of Isidore (Izzy) and Augusta (Gussie) Barnett Miller's three children. His brother Kermit born in 1912, sister Joan 1922.

1920–28   Attends PS 24 in Harlem, then an upper-middle-class Jewish neighbourhood, where his mother went to the same school. The family lives in an apartment overlooking Central Park on the top floor of a six-storey building at 45 West 110th Street, between Lenox and Fifth Avenues. Takes piano lessons, goes to Hebrew school and ice-skates in the park. His Barnett grandparents are nearby on West 118th Street. In summers the extended family rents a bungalow in Far Rockaway. Sees his first play in 1923, a melodrama at the Schubert Theatre.

1928   His father's successful manufacturing business in the Garment District, the Miltex Coat and Suit Company, with as many as 800 workers, begins to see hard times faced with the looming Depression. The family moves from Manhattan to rural Brooklyn, where they live at 1350 East 3rd Street, near Avenue M, in the same neighbourhood as his mother's two sisters, Annie Newman and Esther Balsam. Miller plants a pear tree in the backyard ('All I knew was cousins'). Celebrates his bar-mitzvah at the Avenue M Temple.

1930   Transfers from James Madison High School where he is reassigned to the newly built Abraham Lincoln High School on Ocean Parkway. Plays in the football team and injures his leg in a serious accident that will later excuse him from active military service. Academic record unimpressive, and he fails geometry twice.

1931   Early-morning delivery boy for a local bakery before going off to school; forced to stop when his bicycle is stolen. Works for his father during the summer vacation.

1933   Graduates from Abraham Lincoln High School and registers for night school at City College. He leaves after two weeks ('I just couldn't stay awake').

1933–   Earns $15 a week as a clerk for Chadwick-
  34   Delamater, an automobile-parts warehouse in a run-
          down section of Manhattan that will later become the site
          for the Lincoln Center for the Performing Arts. He is the
          only Jewish employee, and experiences virulent anti-
          Semitism for the first time.

1934   Writes to the Dean of the University of Michigan to
        appeal against his second rejection and says he has
        become a 'much more serious fellow' ('I still can't believe
        they let me in'). Travels by bus to Ann Arbor for the
        autumn semester, with plans to study journalism because
        'Michigan was one of the few places that took writing
        seriously'. Lives in a rooming house on South Division
        Street and joins the *Michigan Daily* as reporter and night
        editor; takes a non-speaking part in a student production
        of Shakespeare's *King Henry VIII*. Moves to an attic room
        at 411 North State Street and works part-time in an off-
        campus laboratory feeding past-prime vegetables to
        thousands of mice.

1936   Writes his first play, *No Villain*, in six days during semester
        break and receives a Hopwood Award in Drama for $250
        using the pseudonym 'Beyoum'. Changes his major to
        English.

1937   Enrols in Professor Kenneth T. Rowe's playwriting class.
        Rewrites *No Villain* as *They Too Arise* and receives a major
        award of $1,250 from the Theatre Guild's Bureau of New
        Plays (Thomas Lanier – later Tennessee – Williams was
        another winner in the same competition). *They Too Arise* is
        produced by the B'nai Brith Hillel Players in Detroit and
        at the Lydia Mendelssohn Theatre in Ann Arbor.
        Receives a second Hopwood Award for *Honors at Dawn*
        when Susan Glaspell is one of the judges. Contributes to
        The Gargoyle, the student humour magazine. Drives his
        college friend Ralph Neaphus east to join the Abraham
        Lincoln Brigade in the Spanish Civil War, but decides not
        to go with him. Months later Neaphus, twenty-three, was
        dead.

1938   Composes a prison play, *The Great Disobedience*, and revises
        They Too Arise as *The Grass Still Grows*. Graduates from the
        University of Michigan with a BA in English. Joins the
        Federal Theater Project in New York to write radio plays
        and scripts.

1939   The Federal Theater Project is shut down by conservative forces in Congress and Miller goes on relief. Writes *Listen My Children* and *You're Next* with his friend and fellow Michigan alumnus Norman Rosten. *William Ireland's Confession* is broadcast on the Columbia Workshop.

1940   Marries Mary Grace Slattery, his college sweetheart at the University of Michigan. They move into a small apartment at 62 Montague Street in Brooklyn Heights. Writes *The Golden Years*, a play about Montezuma, Cortez, and the European conquest and corruption of Mexico. *The Pussycat and the Plumber Who Was a Man* airs on CBS Radio. Makes a trip to North Carolina to collect dialect speech for the Folk Division of the Library of Congress.

1941–43   Works as a shipfitter's helper on the night shift at the Brooklyn Navy Yard repairing battle-scarred war vessels from the North Atlantic fleet. Finishes additional radio plays, including *The Eagle's Nest* and *The Four Freedoms*. Completes *The Half-Bridge*. The one-act *That They May Win* is produced in New York.

1944   Daughter Jane is born. Prepares Ferenc Molnar's *The Guardsman* and Jane Austen's *Pride and Prejudice* for radio adaptation, and continues his own writing for the medium. Tours army camps in preparation for the draft of a screenplay called *The Story of G.I. Joe*, based on news reports written by the popular war correspondent Ernie Pyle (withdraws from the project when his role as author is compromised). Publishes *Situation Normal …*, a book about this experience that highlights the real challenges returning soldiers encountered on re-entering civilian life. Dedicates the book to his brother, 'Lieutenant Kermit Miller, United States Infantry', a war hero. *The Man Who Had All the Luck* opens on Broadway but closes after six performances, including two previews. The play receives the Theater Guild National Award.

1945   Publishes *Focus*, a novel about anti-Semitism and moral blindness set in and around New York. His article 'Should Ezra Pound Be Shot?' appears in *New Masses*.

1946   Adapts *Three Men on a Horse* by George Abbott and John C. Holm for radio.

1947   *All My Sons* opens in New York and receives the New York Drama Critics' Circle Award; the Donaldson Award and the first Tony Award for best author. His son Robert is born. Moves with his family to a house he purchases at 31 Grace Court in Brooklyn Heights. Also buys a new car, a Studebaker, and a farmhouse in Roxbury, Connecticut. Writes the article 'Subsidized Theater' for the *New York Times*.

1948   Builds by himself a small studio on his Connecticut property where he writes *Death of a Salesman*. Edward G. Robinson and Burt Lancaster star in the film version of *All My Sons*.

1949   *Death of a Salesman*, starring Lee J. Cobb, Arthur Kennedy, Cameron Mitchell and Mildred Dunnock opens at the Morosco Theatre in New York on 10 February. Directed by Elia Kazan with designs by Jo Mielziner, it wins the New York Drama Critics' Circle Award, the Donaldson Prize, the Antoinette Perry Award, the Theatre Club Award and the Pulitzer Prize. His essay 'Tragedy and the Common Man' is printed in the *New York Times*. Attends the pro-Soviet Cultural and Scientific Conference for World Peace at the Waldorf-Astoria Hotel to chair a panel with Clifford Odets and Dimitri Shostakovich.

1950   Adaptation of Henrik Ibsen's *An Enemy of the People* produced on Broadway starring Fredric March and Florence Henderson ('I have made no secret of my early love for Ibsen's work'). First sound recording of *Death of a Salesman*. *The Hook*, a film script about graft and corruption in the closed world of longshoremen in the Red Hook section of Brooklyn, fails to reach production after backers yield to pressure from the House Committee on Un-American Activities. *On the Waterfront*, the Budd Schulberg–Elia Kazan collaboration featuring Marlon Brando, changes the setting to Hoboken, New Jersey, but is developed from the same concept, and is released four years later.

1951   Meets Marilyn Monroe. Fredric March in the role of Willy Loman for Columbia Pictures in the first film version of *Death of a Salesman*. Joseph Buloff translates the play into Yiddish; his production runs in New York and introduces Miller's play to Buenos Aires.

1952   Drives to Salem, Massachusetts, and visits the Historical Society, where he reads documents and researches the material he will use in *The Crucible*. Breaks with Kazan over the director's cooperation with HUAC.

1953   *The Crucible* wins the Donaldson Award and the

Antoinette Perry Award when it opens in New York at
the Martin Beck Theatre. Directs *All My Sons* for the
Arden, Delaware, Summer Theatre.

1954   US State Department denies Miller a passport to attend
the Belgian premiere of *The Crucible* in Brussels ('I wasn't
embarrassed for myself; I was embarrassed for my
country'). NBC broadcasts the first radio production of
Death of a Salesman. Mingei Theater stages first Japanese
translation of *Salesman* in Tokyo, where the play is
received as a cautionary tale about the 'salaryman'.

1955   The one-act version of *A View from the Bridge* opens in New
York on a double-bill with *A Memory of Two Mondays*.
HUAC pressurises city officials to withdraw permission
for Miller to make a film about juvenile delinquency set in
New York.

1956   Lives in Nevada for six weeks in order to divorce Mary
Slattery. Marries Marilyn Monroe. Subpoenaed to appear
before HUAC on 21 June, he refuses to name names.
Accepts an honorary degree as Doctor of Humane Letters
from his alma mater, the University of Michigan. Jean-
Paul Sartre writes screenplay for French adaptation of *The
Crucible*, called *Les Sorcieres de Salem*; the film stars Yves
Montand and Simone Signoret. Travels with Monroe to
England, where he meets Laurence Olivier, her co-star in
The Prince and the Showgirl. Peter Brook directs revised two-
act version of *A View from the Bridge* in London at the New
Watergate Theatre Club, as censors determined it could
not be performed in public. 'Once Eddie had been
squarely placed in his social context, among his people,'
Miller noted, 'the myth-like feeling of the story emerged of
itself ... Red Hook is full of Greek tragedies.'

1957   Cited for contempt of Congress for refusing to co-operate
with HUAC. On the steps of the United States Congress,
and with Monroe on his arm, he vows to appeal against
the conviction. Monroe buys all members of Congress a
year's subscription to *I.F. Stone's Weekly*. First television
production of *Death of a Salesman* (ITA, UK). *Arthur Miller's
Collected Plays* is published, and his short story 'The
Misfits' appears in *Esquire Magazine*.

1958–   The US Court of Appeals overturns his conviction
59   for contempt of Congress. Elected to the National
Institute of Arts and Letters and receives the Gold Medal
for Drama.

1961   Miller and Monroe divorce (granted in Mexico on the grounds of 'incompatibility'). *The Misfits*, a black-and-white film directed by John Huston featuring the actress in her first serious dramatic role, is released for wide distribution. Miller calls his scenario 'an eastern western' and bases the plot on his short story of the same name. Co-stars include Clark Gable, Montgomery Clift, Eli Wallach and Thelma Ritter. *The Crucible: An Opera in Four Acts* by Robert Ward and Bernard Stambler is recorded. Sidney Lumet directs a movie version of *A View from the Bridge* with Raf Vallone and Carol Lawrence. Miller's mother, Augusta, dies.

1962   Marries Austrian-born Inge Morath, a photographer with Magnum, the agency founded in 1947 by Henri Cartier-Bresson. Marilyn Monroe, aged thirty-six, dies. His daughter, Rebecca Augusta, is born in September. NBC broadcasts an adaptation of *Focus* with James Whitmore and Colleen Dewhurst.

1963   Publishes a children's book, *Jane's Blanket*. Returns to Ann Arbor to deliver annual Hopwood Awards lecture, 'On Recognition'.

1964   Visits the Mauthausen death camp with Inge Morath and covers the Nazi trials in Frankfurt, Germany, for the *New York Herald Tribune*. Reconciles with Kazan. *Incident at Vichy*, whose through-line is 'It's not your guilt I want, it's your responsibility', opens in New York, as does *After the Fall*. The former is the first of the playwright's works to be banned in the Soviet Union. The latter Miller says 'is not about Marilyn' and that she is 'hardly the play's *raison d'etre*'.

1965   Elected president of PEN, the international organisation of writers dedicated to fighting all forms of censorship. American premiere of the two-act version of *A View from the Bridge* is performed Off-Broadway. Laurence Olivier's production of *The Crucible*, starring Colin Blakely and Joyce Redman, is staged in London at the Old Vic by the National Theatre. Returns to Ann Arbor, where his daughter Jane is now a student, to participate in the first teach-in in the US concerning the Vietnam conflict.

1966   First sound recording of *A View from the Bridge*. In Rome Marcello Mastroianni and Monica Vitti play the parts of Quentin and Maggie in Franco Zeffirelli's Italian production of *After the Fall*. Miller's father, Isidore, dies.

1967   *I Don't Need You Any More*, a collection of short stories, is
        published. Sound recording of *Incident at Vichy*. Television
        production of *The Crucible* is broadcast on CBS. Visits
        Moscow and tries to persuade Soviet writers to join PEN.
        Playwright-in-Residence at the University of Michigan.
        His son, Daniel, is born in January.

1968   *The Price*, which the playwright called 'a quartet', 'the most
        specific play I've ever written', opens on Broadway. Sound
        recording of *After the Fall*. Attends the Democratic National
        Convention in Chicago as a delegate from Roxbury,
        Connecticut. Leads peace march against the war in South-
        East Asia with the Reverend Sloan Coffin, Jr, at Yale
        University in New Haven. *Death of a Salesman* sells its
        millionth copy.

1969   *In Russia*, a collaborative project with text by Miller and
        photography by Morath, is published. Visits Prague in a
        show of support for Czech writers; meets Vaclav Havel.
        Retires as president of PEN.

1970   Miller's works are banned in the Soviet Union, a result of
        his efforts to free dissident writers. *Fame* and *The Reason
        Why*, two one-act plays, are produced; the latter is filmed
        at his home in Connecticut.

1971   Television productions of *A Memory of Two Mondays* on
        PBS and *The Price* on NBC. Sound recording of *An Enemy
        of the People*. *The Portable Arthur Miller* is published.

1972   *The Creation of the World and Other Business* opens at the
        Schubert Theatre in New York on 30 November. Attends
        the Democratic National Convention in Miami as a
        delegate. First sound recording of *The Crucible*.

1973   PBS broadcasts Stacy Keach's television adaptation of
        Incident at Vichy, with Harris Yulin as Leduc. Champions
        the case of Peter Reilly, an eighteen-year-old falsely
        convicted of manslaughter for his mother's murder; four
        years later, all charges are dismissed. *After the Fall* with
        Faye Dunaway is televised on NBC. Teaches mini-course
        at the University of Michigan; students perform early
        drafts of scenes from *The American Clock*.

1974   *Up from Paradise*, musical version of *The Creation of the World
        and Other Business*, is staged at the Power Center for the
        Performing Arts at the University of Michigan. With
        music by Stanley Silverman and cover design by Al
        Hirschfield, Miller calls it his 'heavenly cabaret'.

1977   A second collaborative project with Inge Morath, *In the Country*, is published. Petitions the Czech government to halt arrests of dissident writers. The *Archbishop's Ceiling* opens at the Kennedy Center in Washington, DC. Miller said he wanted to dramatise 'what happens … when people know they are … at all times talking to Power, whether through a bug or a friend who really is an informer'.

1978   *The Theater Essays of Arthur Miller* is published. NBC broadcasts the film of *Fame* starring Richard Benjamin. Belgian National Theatre mounts the twenty-fifth anniversary production of *The Crucible*; this time Miller can attend.

1979   *Chinese Encounters*, with Inge Morath, is published. Michael Rudman directs a major revival of *Death of a Salesman* at the National Theatre in London, with Warren Mitchell as Willy Loman.

1980   *Playing for Time*, the film based on Fania Fenelon's autobiography *The Musicians of Auschwitz*, is broadcast nationally on CBS, with Vanessa Redgrave and Jane Alexander. ('I tried to treat it as a story meaningful to the survivors, by which I mean all of us. I didn't want it to be a mere horror story.') *The American Clock* has its first performance at the Spoleto Festival in South Carolina, then opens in New York with the playwright's sister, Joan Copeland, as Rose Baum, a role based on their mother. Miller sees his play as 'a mural', 'a mosaic', 'a story of America talking to itself … There's never been a society that hasn't had a clock running on it, and you can't help wondering – How long?'

1981   Second volume of *Arthur Miller's Collected Plays* is published. Delivers keynote address on the fiftieth anniversary of the Hopwood Awards Program in Ann Arbor.

1982   Two one-act plays that represent 'the colors of memory', *Elegy for a Lady* and *Some Kind of Love Story*, are produced as a double-bill at the Long Wharf Theatre in Connecticut under the title *2 by A.M.*

1983   Directs *Death of a Salesman* at the People's Art Theatre in Beijing, part of a cultural exchange to mark the early stage of the opening of diplomatic relations between the United States and the People's Republic of China. Ying Ruocheng plays Willy Loman in his own Chinese translation. *I Think About You a Great Deal*, a monologue written as a tribute to Vaclav Havel, appears in *Cross Currents*, University of Michigan.

1984   '*Salesman' in Beijing* is published. The texts of *Elegy for a Lady* and *Some Kind of Love Story* are printed under a new title, *Two-Way Mirror*. Receives Kennedy Center Honors for lifetime achievement. Reworks the script of *The American Clock* for Peter Wood's London production at the National Theatre.

1985   Twenty-five million viewers see Dustin Hoffman play Willy Loman, with John Malkovich as Biff and Kate Reid as Linda in the production of *Death of a Salesman* shown on CBS. Goes to Turkey with Harold Pinter for PEN as an ambassador for freedom of speech. Serves as delegate at a meeting of Soviet and American writers in Vilnius, Lithuania, where he attacks Russian authorities for their continuing anti-Semitism and persecution of *samizdat* writers. *The Archbishop's Ceiling* is produced in the UK by the Bristol Old Vic. Completes adaptation of *Playing for Time* as a stage play.

1986   One of fifteen writers and scientists invited to meet Mikhail Gorbachev to discuss Soviet policies. The Royal Shakespeare Company uses a revised script of *The Archbishop's Ceiling* for its London production in the Barbican Pit.

1987   Miller publishes *Timebends: A Life*, his autobiography. Characterising it as 'a preemptive strike' against future chroniclers, he discusses his relationship with Marilyn Monroe in public for the first time. *Clara* and *I Can't Remember Anything* open as a double-bill at Lincoln Center in New York under the title *Danger: Memory!* Broadcasts of *The Golden Years* on BBC Radio and Jack O'Brien's television production of *All My Sons* on PBS. Michael Gambon stars as Eddie Carbone in Alan Ayckbourn's intimate production of *A View from the Bridge* at the National Theatre in London. University of East Anglia names its site for American Studies the Arthur Miller Centre.

1988   Publishes 'Waiting for the Teacher', a nineteen-stanza free-verse poem, in *Ha'aretz*, the Tel Aviv-based liberal newspaper, on the occasion of the fiftieth anniversary of the founding of the State of Israel.

1990   *Everybody Wins*, directed by Karel Reisz with Debra
       Winger and Nick Nolte, is released: 'Through the evolution
       of the story – a murder that took place before the story
       opens – we will be put through an exercise in experiencing
       reality and unreality.' Television production of *An Enemy of
       the People* on PBS. Josette Simon plays Maggie as a sultry
       jazz singer in Michael Blakemore's London revival of *After
       the Fall* at the National Theatre, where *The Crucible* also
       joins the season's repertory in Howard Davies's production
       starring Zoë Wannamaker and Tom Wilkinson. Updated
       version of *The Man Who Had All the Luck* is staged by Paul
       Unwin in a joint production by the Bristol Old Vic and the
       Young Vic in London.

1991   *The Last Yankee* premieres as a one-act play. *The Ride Down
       Mount Morgan*, 'a moral farce', has its world premiere in
       London: 'The play is really a kind of nightmare.'
       Television adaptation of *Clara* on the Arts &
       Entertainment Network. Receives Mellon Bank Award
       for lifetime achievement in the humanities.

1992   *Homely Girl, A Life* is published with artwork by Louise
       Bourgeois in a Peter Blum edition. Writes satirical op-ed
       piece for the *New York Times* urging an end to capital
       punishment in the US.

1993   Expanded version of *The Last Yankee* opens at the
       Manhattan Theatre Club in New York. Television
       version of *The American Clock* on TNT with the
       playwright's daughter, Rebecca, in the role of Edie.

1994   *Broken Glass*, a work 'full of ambiguities' that takes 'us back
       to the time when the social contract was being torn up',
       has a pre-Broadway run at the Long Wharf Theatre in
       Connecticut; opens at the Booth Theatre in New York on
       24 April. David Thacker's London production wins the
       Olivier Award for Best Play.

1995   Tributes to the playwright on the occasion of his eightieth
       birthday are held in England and the US. Receives William
       Inge Festival Award for Distinguished Achievement in
       American Theater. *Homely Girl, A Life and Other Stories*, is
       published. In England the collection appears under the title
       Plain Girl. Darryl V. Jones directs a production of *A View
       from the Bridge* in Washington, DC, and resets the play in a
       community of Domincan immigrants. The Arthur Miller
       Society is founded by Steve Centola.

1996   Revised and expanded edition of *The Theater Essays of Arthur Miller* is published. Receives the Edward Albee Last Frontier Playwright Award. Rebecca Miller and Daniel Day-Lewis are married.

1997   *The Crucible*, produced by the playwright's son, Robert A. Miller, is released for wide distribution and is nominated for an Academy Award. Revised version of *The Ride Down Mount Morgan* performed at the Williamstown Playhouse in Massachusetts. BBC airs television version of *Broken Glass*, with Margot Leicester and Henry Goodman repeating their roles from the award-winning London production.

1998   *Mr Peters' Connections* opens in New York with Peter Falk. Revival of *A View from the Bridge* by the Roundabout Theatre Company wins two Tony Awards. Revised version of *The Ride Down Mount Morgan* on Broadway. Miller is named Distinguished Inaugural Senior Fellow of the American Academy in Berlin.

1999   Robert Falls's fiftieth anniversary production of *Death of a Salesman*, featuring Brian Dennehy as Willy Loman, moves from the Goodman Theater in Chicago and opens on Broadway, where it wins the Tony Award for Best Revival of a Play. Co-authors the libretto with Arnold Weinstein for William Bolcom's opera of *A View from the Bridge*, which has its world premiere at the Lyric Opera of Chicago.

2000   Patrick Stewart reprises his role as Lyman Felt in *The Ride Down Mount Morgan* on Broadway, where *The Price* is also revived (with Harris Yulin). Major eighty-fifth birthday celebrations are organised by Christopher Bigsby at the University of East Anglia and by Enoch Brater at the University of Michigan, where plans are announced to build a new theatre named in his honour; it opens officially on 29 March 2007 ('whoever thought when I was saving $500 to come to the University of Michigan that it would come to this'). 'Up to a certain point the human being is completely unpredictable. That's what keeps me going … You live long enough, you don't rust.' *Echoes Down the Corridor*, a collection of essays from 1944 to 2000, is published. Miller and Morath travel to Cuba with William and Rose Styron and meet Fidel Castro and the Colombian writer Gabriel García Márquez.

2001   Williamstown Theater Festival revives *The Man Who Had All the Luck*. Laura Dern and William H. Macy star in a film based on the 1945 novel *Focus*. Miller is named the Jefferson Lecturer in the Humanities by NEH and receives the John H. Finley Award for Exemplary Service to New York City. His speech *On Politics and the Art of Acting* is published.

2002   Revivals in New York of *The Man Who Had All the Luck* and *The Crucible*, the latter with Liam Neeson as John Proctor. *Resurrection Blues* has its world premiere at the Guthrie Theatre in Minneapolis. Miller receives a major international award in Spain, the Premio Principe de Asturias de las Letras. Death of Inge Morath.

2003   Awarded the Jerusalem Prize. His brother, Kermit Miller, dies on 17 October. *The Price* is performed at the Tricycle Theatre in London.

2004   *Finishing the Picture* opens at the Goodman Theatre in Chicago. *After the Fall* revived in New York. Appears on a panel at the University of Michigan with Mark Lamos, who directs students in scenes from Miller's rarely performed plays.

2005   Miller dies of heart failure in his Connecticut home on 10 February. Public memorial service is held on 9 May at the Majestic Theatre in New York, with 1,500 in attendance. Asked what he wanted to be remembered for, the playwright said, 'A few good parts for actors.'

Plot

Setting
After the Fall takes place in the 'mind, thought, and memory'
of the protagonist, Quentin. The set is an abstract
representation of his mind, a landscape that Miller describes
as 'neolithic' and 'lava-like'. The mind, the playwright says,
has no colour, but its memories 'are brilliant against the
grayness of its landscape' (3). The stage directions prescribe
a set of three levels, rising to the highest at the back, crossing
in a curve from one side of the stage to the other, and
connected by a stairway in the centre. The one
representational element of the set is the image of a 'blasted
stone tower of a German concentration camp', which Miller
describes as dominating the stage.

In the original production, the set consisted of a series of
bare, asymmetrical platforms, with a ramp at the centre,
and a staircase going from stage left to stage right behind
the platforms. Only the props and furniture necessary to the
play's action were used. The actors were the most important
objects on the stage.

This set is meant to represent the play of memory in
Quentin's mind. The people who have been important in
his life remain quietly on the stage throughout the play, and
then come to life at various times like memories that remain
dormant in the mind until something causes one to think of
them. The major characters consist of Quentin's father,
mother and brother, his two former wives and the woman
he is thinking of marrying, two friends who have been called
to testify before the House Committee on Un-American
Activities (HUAC), the wife of one of them and a former
client Quentin represented in a divorce case. An important
character is an invisible 'Listener', to whom Quentin talks
throughout the play.

Act One

As the play begins, the characters move with seeming randomness on to the stage, sitting down at various places on the platforms. Quentin emerges from the group and comes forwards to shake the hand of the unseen Listener, who would be sitting just beyond the edge of the stage. In Quentin's opening speech to the Listener, he says that he's come to see him because he has a decision to make, and thanks him for giving him two hours. The fact that Quentin assumes that the Listener knows a good deal about his life but has to fill in events from recent years implies that the Listener is a psychotherapist who used to treat Quentin, but hasn't seen him for some time. In earlier drafts, he is identified as a psychoanalyst. Quentin tells him that he is trying to decide whether to commit to marriage with Holga, a step he is reluctant to take until he understands the failure of his first two marriages, to Louise and Maggie. He speaks of the conflict he feels between despair and an irrational hope for the future in his life.

Although the play is not formally divided into scenes, the rest of Act One consists of what amounts to twelve short scenes between Quentin and the other characters, representing important memories that bear on the life-decision he is trying to make. In the first one, he remembers his encounter with Felice, the young woman whose divorce he has handled. He recalls her hopefulness and her desire to 'bless him' for the self-esteem he brought her. In memory, he tells Felice that you never stop loving whoever you love, but in the play's real time, he berates himself for his hypocrisy, saying that he feels his own wives have injured him.

The second scene is Quentin's memory of telling his father, who was recovering from surgery, about his mother's death. His brother Dan is afraid of the effect the news will have on their father, but Quentin insists that he is strong enough to bear it and he deserves to know because 'it belongs to him'. In real time, Quentin wonders whether he is just crueller than his brother. Their father was emotionally devastated by his wife's death, but Quentin comments that it didn't kill him, and a couple of months later he was strong enough to register and vote. Then Quentin briefly recalls Felice. The fact that he noticed after she blessed him that the light fixtures on the wall of his hotel room were at the right height for him to spread his arms out on them as if he were being crucified is an image that recurs several times in the play, along with Felice's blessing.

In the next scene, Quentin remembers being with his new love-interest Holga at the site of a concentration camp. Quentin says he is reluctant to make a promise to her because he doesn't know whether he has lived in good faith. Asking how one can ever be sure of one's good faith, Holga explains her background to him. Growing up in a family with many Nazi officers, she acted as a courier for her godfather, who was involved in a plot to assassinate Hitler, and she spent two years in forced labour. Still, she is not certain of her good faith because she did not reject Germany sooner. Quentin sees that the concentration camp represents a place where there is no appeal, something he feels now, as despair overtakes his hope for the future.

In the next scene, his mother's coffin appears as he remembers the time when, as a boy, he felt her betrayal of his father. As the family prepares to go to a wedding, his mother tells the young Quentin about her own arranged marriage, to an illiterate businessman when she was on the verge of starting college and was seeing a young medical student who shared her love of music and poetry. Even while she says that Quentin's father is a 'wonderful man', she insists that her son follow in her footsteps, not his, imitating her beautiful penmanship and success at school. From his father's conversation on the telephone, it becomes clear that his business affairs have reached a crisis, brought on by the Great Depression. As it dawns on Quentin's mother that her husband has lost not only his business, but also the family's money, including her own bonds, she calls him a moron and an idiot, and talks about a divorce. Later she tries to comfort the crying boy, insisting that she thinks his father is a wonderful man and that she would never say anything against him.

Following this is another memory of the concentration camp. Quentin asks Holga whether she ever feels complicit in this atrocity and she responds, 'no one they didn't kill can be innocent again'(28). Then Holga tells Quentin about losing her memory in a bombing, wandering around the countryside with refugees and being saved from suicide by an old soldier, who brought her home, enabling her memory to return. She says she knows how terrible it is to owe what one can never repay. She tells Quentin about a recurring dream in which she has a child that 'was my life; and it was an idiot'. She tells Quentin that she kisses the child in the dream and says, 'I think one must finally take one's life in one's arms, Quentin'.

This is followed by a brief scene in which Elise, the wife of Quentin's friend Lou, tries to seduce him. Lou talks about his testimony before HUAC, telling Quentin that he has felt guilty about lying on behalf of the Communist Party in the past. Quentin's first wife Louise confronts him about his failure to engage with her as a person, insisting that he treats her as if she doesn't exist. They refer to Quentin's earlier confession that he was briefly attracted to another woman and he talks to the Listener about Louise's claim to innocence, which made her feel superior, and his own inability to feel innocent. This is followed by a short exchange with his mother, in which she again refers to his father's illiteracy and, Quentin says, seeks to make her his 'accomplice' against his father.

The next long scene is a continuation of the scene with Lou. Their friend Mickey arrives and tells Quentin that he, too, has been called to testify before HUAC, but unlike Lou, he plans to name the names of his former party comrades (which will lead to their being blacklisted and called before the committee themselves). He has come to get Lou to agree to let him name his name. After a long speech defending his position, he asks permission from Lou, who refuses and tells him he will be selling him for his own prosperity. Mickey counters by reminding Lou about his lies for the Party and asks whether Lou's soul is all his own; then Mickey leaves. This is followed by Quentin's conversation with Louise in which he says that he is uncertain about reality, she accuses him of failing to see her as 'a separate person' and he counters that she is unable to admit she is ever at fault.

In the next scene Quentin meets Maggie, a telephone operator at his law firm, while he is sitting in the park. In his memory she is a beautiful but clueless young woman, who is ready to go off with a man because he tells her he knows where she can find a discount record store. During their conversation, it becomes clear that Maggie has had an affair with a judge who was also a member of the firm. As she goes off to catch her bus, she is pursued by two men and Quentin gives her money to take a cab instead.

This is followed by Quentin's return home, where it emerges that he has missed a major meeting at the firm while he was in the park, a meeting where the firm's strategy for dealing with his defence of Lou was going to be discussed. Louise refuses to become involved in Quentin's decision about Lou. Quentin tells her about meeting Maggie. When Louise bristles at this, he gets angry and says it would have been easy to make love to Maggie. Louise gets angry and tells him to sleep on the couch, but they are interrupted by a phone call telling them that Lou has killed himself. Quentin tells Louise that Lou said he was the only friend he had left. In real time, the present, Quentin confesses his feeling that Lou sensed he wanted to be free of his connection to him, and admits that he felt some joy that his danger was now over. Act One ends with Quentin's resentment at being relegated to the living room by Louise and the stage images of Holga, arriving with the promise to be made, and Maggie lying in bed breathing laboriously.

Act Two

The second act begins with Quentin waiting for the Listener to return while he thinks of Holga coming to the airport. Louise appears as she was in college, full of hope and planning their future together, followed by the scene of Quentin and Maggie's wedding day. Quentin says he is 'bewildered by the death of love' and his responsibility for it.

He speaks of the key to understanding his life as darkness and power. Brief memories of his feelings of power with Maggie, Holga and his parents follow this.

The first extended scene is an early visit to Maggie, when she shows her infatuation with Quentin because she feels he respects her and takes her seriously. In real time, Quentin comments that this was a fraud, and at some level he believed she was a joke taking herself seriously. Maggie talks about the father who abandoned her and the success of her singing career that she attributes to the respect Quentin had shown her in the park four years earlier. Maggie tells Quentin about her fear of a hallucination of her judgmental mother, and Quentin tells her that she is moral because she's not afraid of the truth, nor is she pretending to be innocent. In real time, Quentin then thinks of his crucifixion pose and his mother's 'betrayal' of him as a child when she abandoned him by going to Atlantic City without telling him. He says he can't mourn for his mother.

In the next scene, Quentin meets Maggie, now a big singing star, who's in disguise, in the park. She says she wants to meet Quentin in Washington, where he has to accompany a client who is testifying before HUAC, and agrees with his description of her as 'all love'. She shows him her will, which leaves everything to her agent. He is very concerned about this, but says he can't advise her. When a crowd of boys manhandles her while trying to get autographs, Quentin takes her away, saying 'It's like they're eating you.' In her apartment, Maggie starts to take off her clothes, but Quentin stops her and advises her to tear up the will, telling her to stand up when she kneels in front of him trying to express her love and gratitude for his concern. In real time he tells the Listener that he was posturing, that she knew the truth of their relationship; he was acting on the lie that she had to be 'saved', because she had been 'chewed and spat out by a long line of grinning men'. Quentin says he wants to live in good faith, curses his former 'fake innocence', and says he is neither innocent nor good.

This scene is followed by a brief memory of the client's refusing to answer the questions posed by HUAC and

Quentin's real-time expression of doubt that one is good merely because one says no to evil. He feels the need to say yes to something. In the next scene, Quentin says yes to Maggie's offer of sex. This is followed by the memory of their wedding day. Maggie tells her dress designer that Quentin has 'saved' her, getting her to write a new will, changing her psychoanalyst and finding her a top-notch vocal coach. But in the course of the scene Maggie's insecurities begin to show, as she confesses some of her past sexual activity, suggesting that Quentin doesn't have to marry her. Quentin reassures her of his love, but tells the Listener that they 'conspired to violate the past'. Then Maggie reveals her jealousy, complaining that Quentin was too demonstrative to a female friend. Maggie walks into the darkness alone, while expressing her determination to be a good wife.

Several short scenes show Quentin's memories of their deteriorating relationship. Maggie decorates extravagantly while Quentin worries about money; Maggie accuses Quentin of not supporting her enough in her career, while Quentin resents spending so much of his time fighting her legal battles; Maggie complains about the way Quentin's mother treats her; Quentin calls Maggie's language vulgar and Maggie accuses him of not wanting to be with her. Finally, while trying to maintain control over his emotions as they argue, Quentin says he is going for a walk. Drunk, Maggie accuses him of being a 'fag'. She dances to try to attract him and asks if he's going to wait till she's old to leave her. Quentin remembers past betrayals – his own of his father and brother, his and Mickey's of Lou, and his mother's of him.

In the long final scene, Quentin returns to their beach cottage from a business trip during which he has been fired from his law firm, only to find Maggie drinking and taking barbiturates. After saving her from falling off the pier, he warns her that he will call the ambulance if she overdoses, so there will be publicity. He feels that he is at the 'edge of a cliff'. He tells her that he has talked to her analyst, who will be coming to decide with her what she should do. Quentin no longer knows how to prevent Maggie from killing herself, and wants to remove what he feels is her motive, revenge against him, by taking himself out of the picture. He says that 'a suicide kills two people'. He is placing the responsibility for her action in Maggie's hands. Maggie asks Quentin about Lazarus, and Quentin says that God saved Lazarus by raising him from the dead, but a man who tried to do that would only be 'reaching for the power'. Maggie asks what 'moral' is, and Quentin says it is to tell the truth, even against yourself, something he has praised her for in the past. Quentin tells Maggie that pills are her version of power, but to save herself she has to admit the truth about her own cruelty, selfishness and hatred. He tells her she can begin to live if she will only see her own hatred instead of insisting on her self-image as 'the sweet lover of all life' (136). Maggie accuses him of responsibility for her wanting to die, telling him about reading a note he had written shortly after their marriage that said, 'The only one I will ever love is my daughter. If I could only find an honorable way to die.' Quentin tries to explain this as an attempt to face the worst thing he felt about himself, that he could not love, but acknowledges that it is far too late to undo the wrong he did her.

As Maggie sinks into unconsciousness, Quentin takes the bottle of pills from her, and she fights him, but he keeps saying, 'You won't kill me!' His memory flashes to his mother outside the bathroom door during what appears to have been an attempt to drown himself in the bathtub after her betrayal of him when he was a boy. As his mother backs into his hands in real time, Quentin begins to strangle her, and he releases her in horror as she sinks to the floor, saying 'Murder?' Maggie says he tried to kill her, but then confuses him with someone named Frank, and says she will call Quentin to defend her. Quentin calls the maid and tells her to call the ambulance. He tells the Listener that they saved her, but admits that he knew she was beginning to suffocate from the barbiturates when they started to argue, but did nothing. He says that he gambled with her life to get his innocence back and that he turned his back on her.

Moving towards the image of the concentration camp tower, he expresses his realisation that 'no man lives who would not rather be the sole survivor of this place than all its finest victims', and asks who can be innocent again 'on this mountain of skulls'. He acknowledges his brotherhood with both the people who died in the camp and the people who built the place. Quentin expresses his realisation that we live, not in Eden, but after the Fall (the Christian original sin of Adam and Eve), and that we are all very dangerous, a realisation that he shares with Holga, who survived the Nazis. Quentin greets each of the other characters as they emerge from his mind and follow behind him towards Holga. The play ends with Holga and Quentin greeting each other.

Commentary

The aesthetic context

After the Fall was the seventh of Arthur Miller's plays to be produced on Broadway, following *The Man Who Had All the Luck* (1944), *All My Sons* (1947), *Death of a Salesman* (1949), his adaptation of Ibsen's *An Enemy of the People* (1950), *The Crucible* (1953), *A Memory of Two Mondays* (1955) and *A View from the Bridge* (1955). When it was produced as the premiere production of New York's Lincoln Center in 1964, Miller had been absent from the theatre for nine years, during his tempestuous marriage to Marilyn Monroe and the four-year period when he was working on the film *The Misfits* (1961), which he wrote as a vehicle for her.

Perhaps because his first Broadway success came with *All My Sons*, a realistic Ibsenesque tragedy that hinges on a social issue, the exposure of war-profiteering, Miller is most often spoken of as a playwright of straightforward social realism. In fact, he considered writing a play in Ibsenesque realism an experiment when he did it. His earlier play, *The Man Who Had All the Luck*, was a dramatic parable that had failed on Broadway partly because of the conventional realism of the production, which was out of harmony with the play's aesthetic. Another play that Miller was working on in the forties was *The Golden Years*, a verse tragedy about Montezuma. Miller's whole career was actually characterised by an original aesthetic approach to each play. In the true spirit of modernism, he was always trying to discover a new dramatic aesthetic and a theatrical idiom that would bring the idea that was in his mind to life most effectively on stage. In *The Crucible* it was the creation of a dialogic idiom that would suggest the seventeenth century without actually using Elizabethan language. In *A View from the Bridge* it was adapting the form of classical Greek tragedy to express the experience of Brooklyn dock workers in the 1950s.

In several ways, *After the Fall* is the realisation of Miller's original vision of *Death of a Salesman*, which he first entitled *The Inside of His Head*. Miller said that he started with the goal of dramatising Willy Loman's way of thinking just as his mind was breaking down. In creating a dramatic form that expressed this, he broke down the barriers between present and past, reality and 'daydream'. His object was to dramatise the simultaneity of Willy's experience of what is happening to and around him physically, in stage present, with the reality that is running through his mind, which is perhaps even more real to him. To do this, Miller combined the straightforward social realism that he had used in *All My Sons* with expressionism, a European theatrical idiom that had been devised to dramatise a dream or nightmare, with all its distortions, fragmentations and ruptures in time sequence. The uniqueness of Miller's vision is the way in which the two styles of theatre intermingle to create the effect of simultaneity that allows the audience to believe that it is experiencing reality as Willy experiences it, actually participating in his subjectivity. Working with the director Elia Kazan and designer Jo Mielziner, who had collaborated on a less radical attempt by Tennessee Williams to introduce subjective experience into a fundamentally realistic drama in *A Streetcar Named Desire* (1947), Miller participated in creating a new form of theatre that became known as 'the American style' in the 1950s.

Miller's idea of revealing the contents of human consciousness through theatrical staging was not worked out well in his original concept for *Salesman*: 'an enormous face the height of the proscenium arch which would appear and then open up, and we would see the inside of a man's head' (*Theatre Essays*, 135). Revisiting this concept in *After the Fall*, Miller makes it clear that the set literally is '*the mind, thought, and memory of Quentin*'. On this set, the characters from every period of Quentin's life can appear and disappear '*instantaneously, as in the mind*' (3) and time is fragmented along the lines of one of Miller's favourite concepts, 'timebends'.

While the action is anchored in the play's 'real time' by Quentin's conversation with the Listener, it is only his memory that provides chronology to the events that are enacted on the stage, reflecting the subjectivity of Quentin's consciousness.

The play marks the full realisation of Miller's modernist experimentation in trying to create a form that dramatises both human consciousness or subjectivity and its inter-relationship with social and familial dynamics. This experimental structure exists in a productive tension with the psychological realism in Miller's approach to character. The frame of the play is a conversation between Quentin and the unnamed 'Listener', presumably his psychoanalyst, while he attempts to makes sense of the complex nexus of feelings, thoughts and memories he is experiencing as he tries to decide whether to embrace the future and marry again. Both overhearing Quentin's conversation with the Listener and watching his memories as they unfold in his mind, the audience participates in his subjective experience of reality.

Stylistically, the play is in one sense very complex, as the reader or viewer tries to work out the identities and relationships of the characters, the time sequences and the relation of memory to present reality. In another sense, it is absolute simplicity, with little in the way of dramatic conventions intervening between the audience and stage reality, once the concept of the stage being the mind of Quentin is made clear.

The autobiographical and social context

After the Fall is embedded in historical events that were inextricably bound up with Miller's personal life. The play is a perfect illustration of Miller's often-repeated saying that human beings exist in society as the fish is in the sea and the sea inside the fish. *After the Fall* is at the same time an intensely autobiographical self-examination in its psychological study of its protagonist, Quentin, and a moral and philosophical commentary on the historical phenomena of the Holocaust, McCarthyism and the Great Depression.

Miller has acknowledged the autobiographical nature of the play, which he began writing in the summer of 1961, as it became clear that his marriage to Marilyn Monroe was over and he was beginning a relationship with Inge Morath, who was part of a team of Magnum photographers on the set of *The Misfits*, the film that Miller had written for Monroe to provide her with a serious acting role, but which proved to be the last straw in their disintegrating marriage. Just as Quentin is deciding whether he can commit himself to Holga in the play, Miller was wrestling with the question of his relationship with Inge and whether he could make a promise to her about the future, given his feelings about his two failed marriages. Growing out of this personal dilemma, the play addresses the larger issues of the need for human connection and the guilt human beings bear for their failure to live up to an ideal of responsibility for one another. Besides his role as husband, Miller used three important relationships in his own life that intersected with major historical events as the arena for examining these issues. The first was the Holocaust, with which he was preoccupied for many years, making it the subject of three other works in addition to *After the Fall – Incident at Vichy*, *Playing for Time* and *Broken Glass*. The Holocaust was an important reality in his experience with Inge, who was deeply affected by it in her own life, growing up as an Austrian living in Nazi Germany.

A second event was the Great Depression, which had been life-changing for the Miller family. His father Isidore had been a prosperous coat manufacturer before the stock-market crash in 1929, when Arthur was fourteen years old. Like many others, Isidore's business was wiped out by the crash, losing the family's money; the family moved from a large apartment on New York's Central Park to a small house in Brooklyn. He spent years afterwards trying to build another business, but never succeeded. While Arthur's elder brother Kermit stayed with his father, dropping out of college to help with his business, Arthur went off to study at the University of Michigan after saving enough money to

pay his tuition. The play addresses his guilt about that as
well as the feeling of complicity he had with his mother's
contempt for his father after his failure in business.

Miller's own test came with the HUAC hearings, during
which the committee demanded that witnesses cooperate
and name the names of people they had associated with in
radical, socialist or progressive activities in the past, so they
too could be called to testify and in many cases blacklisted
from work in certain areas, including Hollywood. When he
was called in 1956, Miller told the committee that he would
not deny any of the political activities that he was accused of
participating in, but would not name others. For his refusal
to answer the committee's questions, he was convicted of
Contempt of Congress, but his conviction was overturned in
the courts. His friend, the director of *After the Fall* and *Death
of a Salesman*, Elia Kazan, had not followed this course when
he was called in 1952, but had chosen to name names, and
was very public in defending his decision, which
precipitated a break between the two men that lasted until
they came together for Kazan to direct the Lincoln Center
premiere of *After the Fall* in 1964. Both Miller and Kazan
acknowledged that the character Mickey is based closely on
Kazan.

Chronologically, Quentin's memory play begins with the
relationship with his mother, centring on two moments of
betrayal, when she goes away on a trip without telling the
small child Quentin, making him feel abandoned, and when
she turns on her husband after finding out that he has lost
all their money. Quentin's final action of attempting to
strangle his mother suggests the degree of rage he has
against her, while he also acknowledges her love and
encouragement. Miller had similarly mixed feelings about
his mother, acknowledging a complicated Oedipal
connection that he examined in psychoanalysis. One thing
that he blamed her for was undermining his father. Like the
mother in the play, Miller's mother Augusta often talked to
him about the opportunities she had given up in accepting
the marriage to Isidore that her family had arranged. Much
better educated and more cultured than her husband, she

made it clear to her children that the finer values were hers, not his, yet she never forgave her husband for his business failure. Although he came to see this as treachery towards his father, Miller acknowledged that his mother's encouragement was an important factor in his determination to accomplish something in the arts and his belief that he could do so. According to Miller, the scene in which Quentin and his brother Dan have to tell their father about their mother's death parallels the scene in life almost exactly. It was Arthur who broke the news of his mother's death to his father, feeling at the same time some pride in giving him the news that he felt belonged to him and some guilt that he was perhaps only able to do it because he was crueller than his brother.

Quentin's three relationships with women are central to the play, as Miller tried to work through his thoughts and emotions about his relationships with his three wives, Mary, Marilyn and Inge. Miller has said that the relationship between Quentin and Louise is based on his first marriage to Mary Grace Slattery, and she confirmed the accuracy of the portrait to Miller's biographer, Christopher Bigsby, in 2001.

The end of Miller's first marriage came with his relationship with Marilyn Monroe. Perhaps because she was the most famous of the people on whom the play was based, the resemblance between the play's Maggie and Marilyn Monroe was noticed immediately when the play premiered in 1964. Like Maggie, Marilyn was an arrestingly attractive woman who had been damaged emotionally in childhood and exploited in youth, and who had sabotaged her own promising career as she battled mental illness and drug and alcohol addiction. Although he fought the simplistic identification between Maggie and Marilyn that he saw critics making when the play premiered, he said later that his representation of Maggie was an accurate depiction of Marilyn as he knew her. She died of a drug overdose in 1962, an event which influenced Miller's revision of *After the Fall*, which he was already writing.

Miller met the thirty-seven-year-old photographer Inge Morath on the set of *The Misfits*, where she was sent on a photo-shoot by Magnum Photos. As a young girl, she had lived through the Nazi regime in Austria and Germany. After their marriage, they visited the site of the concentration camp at Mauthausen in 1961, an incident Miller uses to frame the larger meaning of his play.

Miller's own collision with history came with the HUAC hearings, which targeted people in show business, particularly the film industry, between 1947 and 1952. Originally set up as a special committee in the 1930s to look into domestic 'Un-American activities' related to fascism and Nazism as well as communism, after the Second World War the Committee was co-opted by several right-wing congressmen and, together with the Senate subcommittee chaired by Joseph McCarthy, became the main enforcer of what has come to be called McCarthyism. Although being a member of the Communist Party has never been illegal in the United States and the party has never sponsored any acts of terrorism, McCarthy and HUAC succeeded in connecting communism and Marxism with domestic terrorism in the public mind. They conducted a series of Congressional Hearings, focusing on show business, labour unions and higher education, in which they subpoenaed people whom they suspected of affiliations with communism or Marxism, either in the present, or in many cases as long as twenty years in the past, and interrogated them about their activities, ostensibly to obtain information about the danger that the threat of communism posed to the public. These hearings exposed no terrorist rings or plots to destroy the country. Instead they performed a subtler function of outing radicals and former radicals, causing them to be blacklisted in several industries, including the movie and television industries, so they couldn't find employment for many years.

HUAC's method was to ask the witness the famous question, 'Are you now, or have you ever been, a member of the Communist Party?' For the most part, witnesses either took advantage of the US Constitution's Fifth Amendment, which provides protection against self-incrimination, and refused to answer, which got them blacklisted by their employers, or answered the questions, which showed that they were 'friendly witnesses' to the committee and they were eventually dismissed and allowed to keep their jobs, although they faced ostracism by a populace which lived in fear of the 'Red Menace' during these early years of the Cold War with the Soviet Union. The committee demanded proof of loyalty from the witnesses before they were dismissed, however, and this is what caused the moral dilemma for Arthur Miller and many other witnesses. The proof was that they would be willing to name the names of others who were involved in Leftist activities, which could be anything from attending meetings of Marxist groups, to marching in May Day parades, to donating to aid funds for the Loyalists in the Spanish Civil War in the 1930s, to signing petitions to eliminate HUAC. These people would then be called before the committee and interrogated, continuing the cycle. It didn't matter that no subversive plots were uncovered or that the same people were named dozens of times. The committee insisted that its hearings were necessary to carry out its charge of investigating subversive activities.

For people on the Left, the demand to name names became the ultimate test of morality. Would you name the names to keep yourself and your family from harm, thus bringing harm to your friends and fellow Leftists? Most went into the hearings believing that it would be wrong to do so, and found that the situation tested their moral mettle. Others welcomed the opportunity to denounce communism, which they had long since rejected, and turned in their former comrades to the committee. Arthur Miller was in the first camp, while Elia Kazan was in the second.

Miller's own testimony came in 1956, after Joseph McCarthy had been censured by the Senate and the popular hysteria he and HUAC had stirred up was dying down. Miller was called before a hearing that was an investigation not of show business but of the misuse of passports, a subject that he was not asked about during his testimony. When asked about his earlier activities, Miller said that he would take the committee's word for anything for which they had evidence, but when asked to name names, he told the committee, 'I want you to understand that I am not protecting the Communists or the Communist Party. I am trying to, and I will, protect my sense of myself. I could not use the name of another person and bring trouble on him.'[1] Perhaps no one was better prepared for this interrogation than the writer of *The Crucible* and he did not waver from his position, nor did he seek the shelter of the Fifth Amendment. He was willing to go to jail for this principle, and he was in fact convicted of Contempt of Congress – the only crime the committee could accuse him of being his refusal to answer their question. It was only the fact that this was so late in HUAC's career that saved Miller from jail, for the courts were now throwing out a number of these contempt citations and Miller's was one of them.

In 1962, when Miller wrote *After the Fall*, he was trying to make sense of what had happened in the previous decade, both on the personal level to alienate him from one of his closest friends, and on the national level to so greatly divide American society in such a short time. In creating the character of Mickey, Miller tried to give voice to Kazan's position as he thought he would express it, in an effort to understand what could motivate the decision he had made. And he seems to have succeeded. While directing the play, Kazan had no problem accepting the version of him that Miller had created.

The basis of the character of Lou is less obvious than that of Mickey but just as personal. One of the people who was ruined by HUAC was the poet Louis Untermeyer. When Miller knew him, Untermeyer was in his sixties, well known for his criticism and poetry anthologies as well as his own poetry, and a close friend of American poets such as Robert Frost, William Carlos Williams and Marianne Moore. In 1950, through the influence of a former student who became a television producer, he became a contestant on the popular quiz show *What's My Line?* where his quick wit

[1] 84th Congress, Investigation of the use of un-Authorized US Passports, Part 4, Arthur Miller Testimony, 21 June 1956.

made him an audience favourite. In 1951, after he was named by a HUAC witness, Untermeyer was fired from the show because the sponsor objected to the negative publicity. A man who had felt he was loved by the many Americans who watched the show was suddenly 'thrown into the street, abolished'. Miller said that 'this was one of the feeds that went into the central theme of *After the Fall*' (*Timebends*, 264).

Themes

In his autobiography *Timebends*, Miller wrote about re-reading Albert Camus' novel *The Fall* in 1960 at the request of a Hollywood producer who had asked him to write a screenplay based on the novel. Nothing came of that project but Camus' novel struck a deep chord with Miller. Camus' anti-hero, 'a self-described "judge-penitent"', as Miller said, is guilty of failing to come to the aid of a girl he saw jump off a bridge into a river. Aside from the fact that the novel 'is about trouble with women', Miller was captivated by Camus' portrayal of the philosophical dilemma of 'how one can ever judge another person once one has committed the iniquitous act of indifference to a stranger's call for help' (ibid., 484). His guilt about his relationship with Marilyn Monroe is clear in his explanation of what he felt was the novel's failure to pursue the implications of the subject, 'something perhaps worse than mere indifference to a call for help':

> What if the man, at risk to himself, had attempted her rescue and then discovered that the key to her salvation lay not in him, whatever his caring, but in her? And perhaps even worse, that strands of his own vanity as well as his love were entwined in the act of trying to save her? Did disguised self-love nullify the ethical act? Could anyone, in all truth, really save another unless the other wished to be saved? Was not the real question how to evoke that wish? And if it refused evocation, when did one confess failure? And how was failure justified, or could it be? *The Fall*, I thought, ended too soon, before the worst of the pain began.
>
> Finally, suicide might not simply express disappointment with oneself but hatred for someone else. (Ibid.)

These ethical questions form the basis of Miller's early thinking as it informed *After the Fall*. Its beginning was the existential dilemma of whether to take action or not.

As he worked on the play, from the summer of 1961 until its premiere in 1964, and in later revisions, these questions remained significant, particularly to the second act where Quentin's relationship with Maggie, and related thematic concerns become more central to the play. The most obvious one is contained in the title. The play takes place *after* the Fall, when the dream of prelapsarian innocence is gone, and, like Adam and Eve driven from the Garden of Eden after their sin, which was eating the fruit of the Tree of Knowledge of Good and Evil, human beings are forced to face the fact that they are guilty of doing bad things and have to find a way to live with that knowledge. In the play's thematic terms, to protest one's innocence of wrongdoing is to reveal one's lack of self-knowledge and failure to face the truth. The main representative of this state in the play is Louise, who, with her conviction of moral righteousness, refuses even to entertain the idea that she might be at fault for anything in her deteriorating marriage to Quentin. Maggie also exemplifies this state of mind with her belief in her own existential condition as an innocent victim. And Quentin shares a desire for a belief in his own innocence, longing to return to a time when he could believe that morality was black and white, when it was possible to characterise people as good or bad.

The counterpart of letting go of one's claim to innocence is embracing the search for truth that Quentin defines as morality in the play. Though Quentin mistakenly believes that Maggie is able to tell the truth, even 'against herself' early on, he finds that both Louise and Maggie fail to confront the truth in any fundamental way. Lou, another self-described victim, also violates the truth, both in his conscious lies and in his evasion of his own motives and feelings. Quentin is determined to face the truth of his own evil, no matter where it leads, and it leads finally to his awareness that he is capable of murder, of letting Maggie die to save himself.

The awareness of his capacity for evil leads to a further epiphany for Quentin, the thematic thread that has been the most difficult for the play's audiences and reviewers to accept, that of complicity. The guard tower hovers over the play as a reminder that, in Quentin's words, 'I am not alone, and no man lives who would not rather be the sole survivor of this place than all its finest victims.' Taking this one step further, he asks, 'Who can be innocent again on this mountain of skulls? . . . My brothers died here . . . but my brothers built this place; our hearts have cut these stones!' (143–4). In a sense, this is Miller's formulation of the concept of original sin. In biblical terms, Adam and Eve sinned, making the human race guilty ever after. In Miller's play, Quentin discovers in his own capacity for evil his kinship with the rest of humankind. He forces on the audience the question of who can live in a world where such evil as genocide happens – as it continues to do over and over again – do nothing about it, and claim to be innocent of evil?

In 1964 Miller's audience was not ready to discuss, or even to hear, the idea that all who did not die in the Holocaust have some measure of responsibility for it, or that the guilt for this abomination is forgivable. In hindsight, it is not surprising that the critics responded in the way they did to the play, although they might not have been fully aware of the source of their reaction. In the years afterwards, Miller continued to develop and refine his thinking about the subject, in plays that have proved just as unsettling for audiences, without deviating from the fundamental contention that the Holocaust is only one horrific instance of the human capacity for evil in which we all share and that we must recognise this capacity in ourselves as well as in others, and be prepared to forgive the evil actions that both we and others commit. Blindly claiming innocence for ourselves, as Louise and Maggie do, and pretending that evil is the doing of some demonised Other, from which we can distance ourselves with such epithets as 'inhuman' and 'monstrous', is, in Miller's view, an evasion of the moral reality with which human beings must grapple.

As to the question of how to live with the knowledge that 'we meet unblessed; not in some garden of wax fruit and painted trees, that lie of Eden, but after, after the Fall, after many, many deaths' (144), Miller affords some hope in Quentin's embracing of the truth. 'The wish to kill is never killed, but with some gift of courage one may look into its face when it appears and with a stroke of love . . . forgive it; again and again . . . forever?' In Quentin, Miller represents redemption through seeing the truth about one's own guilt and accepting it, yet choosing to live in the world, to embrace the future, to try once again to love despite the knowledge of hatred.

Characters

Quentin

Quentin is the only character in the play who is meant to be seen as a fully rounded, psychologically 'real' person. The other characters exist only in his memory, and, as memories, they are shaped and distorted both by Quentin's view of them at the time the events he is remembering took place and by his memory of them. Their character traits are exaggerated by his feelings for the characters and the situation. For example, his memory of his brother Dan is as the personification of the 'good son' in contrast to himself, the son who abandoned the family. Dan is depicted as selfless, sacrificing everything for the family, even giving Quentin his beloved volume of Byron's poetry and his new argyle socks when he departs for college, leaving Dan, who has abandoned education to help his father, to cope with the family's problems. All of Dan's brief scenes in the play exhibit some form of his moral superiority over Quentin. Felice is a similarly one-dimensional character. She comes into the play only to show her hero-worship of Quentin, to thank him for 'saving' her by making her believe in herself, enabling her to succeed as a professional dancer after her divorce. The recurring image of Felice with her hand up blessing him represents the impact that she had on

Quentin's consciousness. To Quentin she represents all the
women who had faith in his power to help them, from
Louise at the beginning, to Maggie, but who inevitably are
disappointed because they place him in the false position of
Christ-like saviour, which he knows he can never live up to.
The opposite of Felice is Elsie, the figure of temptation, a
combination of Eve and the snake in the garden of Eden.
His recurrent memory of her standing before him and
letting her robe drop to reveal her naked breasts shows her
as the image of sexual temptation. Her behaviour is worse
because she is betraying her best friend Louise and her
husband Lou at the same time. Mickey also says she is
responsible for having forced Lou to lie and betray his own
sense of integrity when he wrote his book about the Soviet
Union, throwing his true book in the fireplace and making
him write a false one. Thus Elsie becomes a representation
of the danger and the treachery that Quentin sees in
women, but also evokes his sense of his own evil, as he says,
'it isn't only that Elsie tempted me, it's worse. If I see a sin
why is it in some part mine?'(39).

As the protagonist, Quentin defines the action of the play.
It is informed by his desire to face the truth and to clarify his
life. In order to decide whether to make a commitment to
Holga, he has to answer the question whether he is capable
of truly loving another person, whether he has the hope and
faith in the future to begin a new life with her. After what
he's been through in his two marriages, he feels that 'it's
outrageous to think of committing myself again' and that
he's a little afraid of 'who and what I'd be bringing to her'
(5). He tells the Listener that every morning he still feels the
hope that he felt as a boy, but it is quickly dampened by
what he feels is the pointlessness of his life. Part of his
motivation for the re-examination of his life is to try to
'corner that hope, find what it consists of, and either kill it
for a lie or really make it mine' (6), so that he can get on
with his life.

Quentin's memory is defined by an oppositional dynamic of
resentment and guilt. On the one hand, as he thinks back over
his marriages, he is overcome by the feeling that 'these

goddamned women have injured me' (7). His memories of
them are imbued with his anger at their treatment of him. But
his memories also bear the weight of his own guilt, his sense
that he was as much at fault as they. 'I am bewildered by the
death of love,' he says, 'and my responsibility for it' (80).

Mother

The fact that Quentin's mother appears several times
throughout the play to say the words 'you idiot' and 'my
bonds' suggests that her strongest impact on Quentin is
related to what he feels is her betrayal of his father. The
scene that he witnessed as a boy, when it became clear that
his father had lost not only his business but also the family's
money, including his life insurance and the bonds that were
meant to provide for his wife's security, has clearly been a
defining one for Quentin. His mother's immediate reaction
on learning of her husband's business decisions is etched in
his memory: 'You mean you saw everything going down
and you throw good money after bad? Are you some kind of
a moron? . . . You are an idiot!' (26–7). She goes on to say
that she should have run the day she met him, she never
should have agreed to her arranged marriage with him, she
should get a divorce. As a reaction to the news in the heat of
the moment, and one incident in a long marriage in which
her husband refers to her as his 'right hand' (13), this might
be put into context as not very important, but it clearly was
a defining moment for her son. Even though she tries to
reassure the crying boy, telling him, 'I was a little angry,
that's all, but I never said that. I think he's a wonderful
man!', Quentin sees her as betraying his father by
undermining him in this way. What's more, he feels that she
has made him her 'accomplice' by belittling his illiterate
father and making him feel that he should share her
superior values. She tells him that she discovered her
husband's illiteracy when he handed her the menu to read
two weeks after their wedding, a treacherous thing to say to
'a little boy . . . who knows how to read; a powerful reader,
that little boy!' (39).

Quentin feels that his mother has betrayed him as well, making him feel that he was the centre of her world, and then, as it seemed to a young child, deserting him by going away for a week without telling him. Having seen a falling star shortly after Quentin's birth, she tells him, 'suddenly it fell, like some great man had died, and you were being pulled out of me to take his place, and be a light, a light in the world!' (83). She not only placed impossible expectations on her son, but the exaggerated sense of his own importance that she gave him made it difficult for him to behave in a mature way in his relationships with women. Although Quentin resents this aspect of his mother, which he has come to see as destructive, he also understands that she gave him something positive too. Her emphasis on his education enabled him to insist on going to college despite the feeling that he should have stayed at home to help his father with the business, and to become a successful lawyer. Her belief in him also helped him to maintain his feelings of self-worth: 'she was a light to me whenever it was dark. I loved that nut, and only love does make her real and mine' (108). In the end, he is forced to accept the complexity of his feelings towards his mother, putting his hands around her throat when she appears during his final scene with Maggie, and then releasing her in horror, saying 'Murder?' (141). It is love and hatred mixed, a nexus of feelings that he has to accept when he recognises himself as someone who lives 'after the Fall'.

Louise

In the case of his traditional marriage to Louise, Quentin realises that he was so absorbed in himself and his work that he has failed to see her as an individual, to listen to her, to take an interest in her. As she says, he acts as if 'I don't . . . *exist*. People are supposed to find out about each other. I am not all this uninteresting, Quentin' (36). Quentin thinks that reading his legal briefs to her is engaging in conversation. She complains that what he wants from her is constant attention and praise for his work. In other words, this is not a relationship of equals, but one in which he makes the emotional demands and she attends to them, a relationship that Louise inevitably tires of, and that she rejects once she goes into analysis and begins to recover her self-confidence.

Quentin clearly feels guilt for the interest in other women that was the flip side of his lack of interest in Louise, but his memory is coloured by his resentment of her as he tries to justify his behaviour and insist that she bore part of the blame. He was surprised that she 'didn't get over it for six months' when he told her, after they had been married a year, that he had been attracted to another woman but did nothing about it. Although he realises later that 'it was an idiotic thing to tell you', he insists that 'I mean it as a compliment; that I did not touch her because I realized what you mean to me', and blames her for treating him 'as though I were some kind of a monster who could never be trusted again' (38). Louise denies that her reaction was this extreme, but Quentin later insists that he was 'forever on trial' in their marriage, and tries to get her to admit some responsibility for his behaviour when he did have an affair with another woman: 'Are you an innocent bystander here? I keep waiting for some contribution you might have made to what I did, and I resent not hearing it' (52). He accuses her of turning her back on him in bed and says that his affair was the result of his feeling 'like nothing'.

Maggie

As Quentin's memory spins out, it becomes clear that he never fully absorbed what Louise was trying to tell him. When he meets Maggie in the park, he comes home and tells her about it, perhaps in some sense a retaliation for her insistence that he is guilty of being unfaithful and her own statement that 'I don't do things I'm ashamed of' (70). Quentin insists that the experience of meeting Maggie made him want to come home to Louise 'full of love'. When Louise reacts with resentment and banishes him to sleep in the living room, Quentin is surprised and devastated that his daughter will know about the trouble between her parents.

In real time, he confesses to his own moral confusion: 'What the hell is moral? What does that really mean? And what am I . . . to even ask that question? A man ought to know . . . a decent man knows that like he knows his own face!' (72–3). Yet he still resents Louise's failure to doubt her own righteousness and her unwillingness to consider his motives or his confusion.

Quentin's greatest source of guilt, of course, is his relationship with Maggie. His final confession to the Listener that he was willing to let her die, that he listened to the breathing that told him she had already overdosed on barbiturates and didn't act immediately to save her, that in a sense, 'I know how to kill' (143), is the central confession of the play. It leads to his final sense of brotherhood with the builders of the death camps and his realisation that he can never be innocent again. It is this fact of human evil, and his own participation in it, that he finally must forgive. It is a forgiveness that liberates him to embrace the future with Holga, who also recognises her own connection with evil and the necessity to live with it, rather than to keep protesting one's innocence, as Louise does.

There are other moments of recognition that lead to this epiphany and, as he does with Louise, Quentin balances his own sense of guilt with his resentment of Maggie's claim to innocence. His crucial sin against her was his failure to be truthful with her, even as he was praising her for being truthful about herself. He allows her to think that he doesn't try to have sex with her when they first meet out of respect, when in fact he is simply afraid to make a move. 'The first honor was that I hadn't tried to go to bed with her! God, the hypocrisy! . . . Because, I was only afraid, and she took it for a tribute to her . . . "value"!' (90). Looking back, he believes that his relationship with Maggie began to go wrong when he was not honest about his physical attraction to her when she first offered him sex and instead gave her advice about her will, telling her, 'you're straight, you're serious, you're first-class' (105). 'She had the truth that day, I brought the lie that she had to be "saved"! From what – except my own contempt?' (104). Placing himself in the role of noble saviour

who wants nothing for himself from the relationship puts
Quentin in bad faith with Maggie from the beginning.
Because of this deception, their relationship is based on her
idealised conception of who he is and his attempt to live up
to this false image.

In his memories, Quentin sees the same bad faith in
Maggie. When he meets her, he finds her refreshing because
she doesn't make the same claims to innocence that Louise
does. He believes that she has the one word 'Now!' written
on her forehead, which he takes as a liberation from the
burden of the future. When he tells her in wonderment that
she seems to be 'all love', she responds, 'That's all I am! A
person could die any minute you know!' (99). Finally,
despite his sense of shame about her sexually promiscuous
past, he believes her to be inherently moral because she
seems to meet his main criterion for this: 'You tell the truth,
even against yourself. You're not pretending to be . . .
innocent' (93). Thus she seems to be everything Louise is
not – warm, loving, sexually free and unashamed, honest,
happily embracing life in the present without claims to
moral superiority. But this proves to be as much of a pose as
Quentin's own nobility. What he doesn't see is the damaged
side of Maggie's character, which she keeps carefully hidden
until after they are married.

Along with her drug and alcohol dependency, Maggie's
insensitivity and cruelty emerge in time, as well as her
selfishness, her self-destruction and, centrally, her
conception of herself as victim and her hatred for the rest of
the world, eventually including Quentin, for persecuting
her. In the end, Maggie turns out to be much like Louise in
that she perceives herself as an ultimately innocent victim
and refuses to entertain any thoughts of her own guilt. This
requires that she see Quentin as the representation of evil.
In the end, as she threatens suicide, he asks her, 'Do you
know who I am? Aside from my name? I'm all the evil in the
world, aren't I? All the betrayal, the broken hopes, the
murderous revenge?' (131). He believes that she was setting
him up to be a murderer by making him responsible for her
suicide and he challenges her to face the truth that he

believes will save her, to 'see [your] own hatred, and live!' (136). Of course this is impossible for Maggie at this point in her life but it gives Quentin some sense of relief.

For his part, Quentin is able to admit that his feeling for Maggie is not simply grief, because 'there's too much hatred in it' (96). When he re-examines their relationship, he realises that his desire to 'save' her was really a desire for power, a desire he also felt in exerting his influence over Felice. When Maggie compares herself to Lazarus, whom Jesus raised from the dead, Quentin sees his own attempt to usurp the power that belongs only to someone larger than life. 'God's power is love without limit,' he says, 'But when a man dares reach for that . . . he is only reaching for the power' (134–5). Limitless love by human beings is a lie, a lie that 'throws a shadow on the face of God'. In the end, his pose of 'saving' Maggie was not only an attempt to exert power over her but also another instance of his dishonesty towards her.

Quentin's confrontation with his own failings helps him towards a clarification of the morality he seeks. Early in the play, he speaks nostalgically to the Listener of the time in his youth when morality seemed clear: 'Remember? When there were good people and bad people? And how easy it was to tell! The worst son of a bitch, if he loved Jews and Negroes and hated Hitler – he was a buddy. Like some kind of paradise compared to this' (29–30). The action of the play is in one sense Quentin's revisiting of his simplistic notions of morality. He admits to having judged others harshly when he was young, but as he faces his own betrayals of Louise and Maggie, he loses faith in his own standards of goodness and his ability to define what is moral. Finally, he seems to come down to the principle of truth that he enunciates to Maggie. He rejects Louise's idea of 'decency' and tells the Listener that he has come to believe that 'decency is murderous'. His resolve is to 'speak truth, not decency – I curse the whole high administration of fake innocence!' (105). He proclaims the fact that he is neither innocent nor good, that he has not lived up to his standard of truth. He confesses that he has lived in bad faith.

Holga

It is Holga's lack of certainty in her own good faith that draws Quentin to her. When he confesses to her that what keeps him from making promises about the future is that he is not sure that he has lived in good faith, she replies, 'But how can one ever be sure of one's good faith?' (18). After she tells him about her experiences with the Nazis and her own moral uncertainty because she had lived so long in Germany without doing anything to resist them, he blesses her uncertainty and tells her how much he values the fact that she is not constantly seeking a moral victory over him. In Quentin's consciousness, Holga doesn't assume the complexity that Maggie and Louise do, but is closer to characters like Dan and Felice, who embody particular qualities that Quentin associates with them. What Holga stands for is the ability to embrace one's life, despite one's moral uncertainty, and go on. The dream she has of kissing the 'idiot child' that is her life and accepting it represents her willingness to do this. It is the example of Holga that gives Quentin licence to do the same.

Lou and Mickey

Lou and Mickey represent the two opposing sides in the moral struggle occasioned by the HUAC hearings. Lou is the test of Quentin's loyalty and courage. Defending Lou was doing what Quentin believed to be right and he stands by him to the end. But in this action, which even Louise admires as morally courageous, Quentin sees his own guilt. Quentin refers to the day he found out that Lou had been dishonest, that he had lied in his books to support the communist line, as 'the day the world ended, it all fell down, and nobody was innocent again' (33). The realisation that what he was defending in representing Lou was morally tainted ended Quentin's illusions of absolute morality and his own innocence. His actions became no longer about abstract principles of right and wrong, but about his behaviour towards other human beings. When Lou told him that he was his most loyal friend, Quentin comes to see he was not praising him but begging him to be his friend, to continue to defend him. And Quentin admits that, though he thinks he would have 'stuck it to the end', he 'hated the danger in it' (74) for himself, and that Lou had seen that. In a further admission, Quentin admits to feeling 'that joy when a burden dies' when Lou killed himself. It is facing that truth about himself that allows him to understand how the contractors, the carpenters and the plumbers could have co-operated in building the site for mass murder in the concentration camp: 'good fathers, devoted sons, grateful that someone else will die, not they'. Quentin comes to feel that no one can understand the reality of evil who is 'innocent; if somewhere in the soul there is no accomplice' (75).

Like Quentin, Mickey has a desire to acknowledge what he sees as his past sins and to honour the truth. He believes that his motive for wanting to testify before HUAC is that he wants 'to live an open life, a straightforward, open life!' He tells Lou, 'a man's got to take the rap . . . for what he's done, for what he is. I think what you hide poisons you' (44–5). Lou agrees with him until he learns that Mickey's plan for doing that also involves informing on others, including Lou. He accuses Mickey of 'selling me for your own prosperity' (47), since he will surely be fired from the university where he teaches if he is named before HUAC. But when he exclaims that 'they have bought your soul!' Mickey counters with 'And yours? Lou! Is it all yours, your soul?' Of course Lou has just acknowledged that his soul is not completely his own by admitting that he had lied to follow the Party line in his writing, and Mickey knows that he folded under pressure from Elsie to tell those lies.

Lou and Elsie call Mickey a monster and a 'moral idiot', but the truth for Quentin is not as simple as that. He remembers a long speech of self-defence in which Mickey makes some plausible arguments for his position: that there is no reason to protect the Communist Party, which they have all despised for many years; that he has no 'solidarity' with the people he could name apart from Lou, and hence no reason for loyalty to them; that the love between him and Lou was born of a respect for truth and a hatred of hypocrisy, and he would be betraying both by not being true to himself now; that not testifying might allow him to keep Lou's friendship, but it would cause him to betray his own sense of self because he really believes that the Communist Party is a conspiracy; that they can't keep turning their backs on the truth 'simply because reactionaries are saying it' (46). Some of these arguments have more merit than others, but it is telling that, in his memory, Quentin gives Mickey his say. If the day he realised that Lou was not innocent was the day the world ended, it was also the day that he acknowledged that Mickey was not simply a monster or a moral idiot, but a man like himself, who struggled with his own sense of what was right even if he made a choice that Quentin found morally wrong. In the end, Mickey is represented as sacrificing Lou for his own well-being. It may not have been in such crass terms as Lou suggests, but whether it was for material or spiritual comfort, or a little of both, it was a selfish act. Mickey finally represents a drive for self-preservation, something that Quentin finds that he shares, in his feeling of relief at Lou's death and, more profoundly, his willingness to let Maggie die.

Productions

The premiere

The premiere performance of *After the Fall* on 23 January 1964 was a significant event in the history of the American theatre for more than one reason. First, it marked the return of Arthur Miller to the New York stage with a new play. It had been nine years since the production of *A View from the Bridge* and expectations were high. This production was also the opening theatrical production for New York's Lincoln Center for the Performing Arts, an ambitious new space including venues for opera, ballet, music concerts and theatre. The Lincoln Center Repertory Theatre was originally conceived as a national company along the lines of Britain's National Theatre. The co-director of the

Repertory Theatre, along with the producer Robert
Whitehead, was Elia Kazan, who had been chosen for his
position both because of his successful record as a Broadway
director and for his experience in working with companies
of actors, both in the Group Theatre when he was young,
and later as a co-founder of the Actors Studio. The choice
of directors was controversial. While no one doubted their
talent or their record of success, several critics thought that
hiring them was bringing the commercial standards and the
mercenary values of Broadway to what was supposed to be
an artistic alternative to it.

The choice of a new play by Arthur Miller as the theatre's
first production might seem to be fairly safe. After all, he
had a steady stream of plays that were both commercially
successful and artistically renowned, including *Death of a
Salesman*. There was, however, the issue of Miller's
relationship with Kazan and the question of whether they
could work together again after the break in their friendship
and working relationship following Kazan's HUAC
testimony. In the end, their relationship proved not to be a
problem for the work. While they did not achieve anything
like the closeness they had felt in working on *Death of a
Salesman* or *All My Sons*, they achieved a solid professional
collaboration during the preparations for *After the Fall*.

In taking on the play Kazan was in the peculiar position
of directing a work for which he had a complicated personal
relationship not only with the playwright but also with the
autobiographical sources for several of the characters as
well. Since Quentin's life is very much modelled on Miller's,
Kazan as director treated him as a projection of the
playwright and developed his characterisation according to
his own view of Miller. Since Kazan had had an affair with
Marilyn Monroe himself, he felt that he understood the
character of Maggie intimately. Even more direct was his
relationship with Mickey, who, he knew, was modelled on
him. Thus, as director he was in the position of interpreting
a character who essentially embodied Arthur Miller's
judgement of his actions in testifying before HUAC, actions
that he knew Miller disapproved of but which both he and

Miller said they never discussed in the course of their many pre-production conferences on the script or during the three-month rehearsal period.

Since everyone involved was avidly committed to the idea of a repertory theatre, the preparation for the production was much longer and more intense than that on any Broadway play the two artists had worked on before. Instead of the usual Broadway rehearsal period of three and a half weeks, preceded by a few consultations, script conferences and letters between playwright and director, the process for *After the Fall* began in the summer of 1963, with Miller and Kazan meeting often to discuss Miller's evolving script, which had already been through many revisions. When rehearsals began on 24 October, the script was still not in finished form, but this was not considered a major problem since three months had been allowed for rehearsal. At the opening rehearsal, Miller read the script to the company as a work-in-progress, and he made substantial revisions at Kazan's suggestion after the first few rehearsals, and Kazan did his best to realise what he saw as Miller's thematic intention on stage.

Despite his understanding of Quentin's pursuit of the truth as the play's centre, Kazan consistently said that he thought the 'guts' of the play was the second act, and that, after he had asked Miller to go home and revise it one more time, the playwright had bravely exposed the raw truth of his relationship with Monroe. To make a complicated emotional situation even more complicated, Kazan cast Barbara Loden, with whom was having an affair at the time, as Maggie, and not only coached her in a performance that shadowed Marilyn Monroe, but also had her wear a blonde wig that made the resemblance unsettling to many of the audience.

One seeming complication with the production ended up as a blessing. Because the Vivian Beaumont Theater, the Lincoln Center venue for plays, was not going to be completed in time for the opening of the play, Robert Whitehead erected the temporary ANTA-Washington Square Theatre, a bare cement structure that was designed by a long-time collaborator with both Miller and Kazan, the designer Jo Mielziner. It was as if a theatre had been designed expressly for *After the Fall*. The bare, uneven platforms representing Quentin's mindscape were surrounded by the audience on three sides, placing the drama in the midst of the audience and heightening the effect of Quentin's connection to them. So immediate was the connection that none of the reviewers understood that there was supposedly an unseen Listener between them and Quentin, but read his speeches as direct address to the audience. It was generally agreed that the bare, abstract space, painted a deep blue, was perfectly suited to the play. Mielziner designed the set in the most minimalist terms. Aside from the abstract image of the guard tower, the most conspicuous elements were the actors representing the characters who populated Quentin's mind. Only the most essential props and pieces of furniture were placed on the stage to indicate the various 'places' to which Quentin's mind travels in the course of the play. Unfortunately, not many reviewers saw the unifying concept of murder, but they did understand the concept of the stage as the mindscape of Quentin, and most found it a very effective setting for the play.

The production was an unlikely hit. Its run was extended into the following year, eventually reaching 208 performances. Barbara Loden won a Tony award for her performance as Maggie and Jason Robards was nominated for his performance as Quentin. The critical response, however, was mixed, and much of it harsh in its condemnation of Miller. The opening-night newspaper critics were for the most part respectful and appreciative. Some of them clearly understood the basic theme of the play and Kazan's directorial concept. John Chapman wrote in the New York *Daily News* that Quentin is engaged in 'an agonized quest for truth – truth about himself, truth about God and truth about just what are the relations between two persons when each is a separate being' (24 January 1964). Others, however, were unable to see past the spectre of the

recently deceased Marilyn Monroe, viewing the play as at
best an exploitation of Miller's connection to her and at
worst an attack on an icon who could not defend herself.

It was the magazine critics who really savaged the play,
particularly 'young Turks' among them who had opposed
the 'old guard' of Broadway being put in control of the
Lincoln Center's theatre. John Simon referred to the play as
'megalomania combined with hypocrisy' (*Hudson Review* 17,
1964; 234). Robert Brustein, who often attacked Miller's
plays, called *After the Fall* 'a three-and-one-half-hour breach
of taste . . . a shameless piece of tabloid gossip, an act of
exhibitionism which makes us all voyeurs' (*New Republic* 150,
8 February 1965; 26–7). Susan Sontag wrote that it was 'the
most notable example of weak-mindedness around at the
moment'.[2] Faced with this vitriolic *ad hominem* attack, Miller
decided to answer what he saw as the most unfounded
accusations in a short article in *Life* magazine. In this article,
he wrote, somewhat disingenuously, that 'the character of
Maggie, which in great part seems to underlie the fuss, is not
in fact Marilyn Monroe. Maggie is a character in a play
about the human animal's unwillingness or inability to
discover in himself the seeds of his own destruction. Maggie
is in this play because she most perfectly exemplifies the self-
destructiveness which finally comes when one views oneself
as pure victim . . . Maggie is quite obviously treated not only
with respect for her agony but with love.'[3] Addressing the
misperception of the play's meaning that he found even
more troubling, he wrote of the theme:

> If life is to be lived, there must be a recognition of the
> individual's part in the evil he sees and abhors . . . instead of
> taking [this point] to heart, there are those who prefer to turn
> it on its head and interpret Quentin as somehow seeking to
> justify himself, when actually he is in search of his
> responsibility – and discovers it. Evidently this is so unfamiliar

[2] Susan Sontag, 'Going to the theater, etc.' in *Against Interpretation*, London:
Eyre and Spottiswoode, 1967, 140.
[3] Arthur Miller, 'With Respect for Her Agony – But With Love', *Life* (7
February 1964), 66.

an idea to many people that they take the play as an apology.
The play is neither an apology nor the arraignment of others;
quite simply, overtly and clearly, it is a statement of
commitment to one's own actions. Indeed, Quentin's impulse
to feel in some concrete way his own authorship of his life and
his person extends to his taking on guilt even for what he did
not do. (Ibid.)

Miller modified his statements about Maggie over the years,
acknowledging the deep connection between her and Marilyn
Monroe. In his 1987 autobiography *Timebends*, he suggests
that, coming so close to Monroe's death, the play was bound
to fail: 'It was as though the critics had witnessed an actual
domestic quarrel and been challenged to come to Maggie's
rescue.' But in considering the critical response, he said that
he 'could not help thinking that this gleeful and all but total
blindness to the play's theme and its implications was one
more proof that they could not be faced, that it was
impossible to seriously consider innocence lethal',
commenting that, 'it was this kind of denial that had brought
about the play's tragic ending' (534). The debate on these
points has continued in criticism of the play, affecting its
subsequent productions. As Robert Martin wrote in 1995,
'*After the Fall* has become a play of audience
misunderstanding, and represents a sad failure by critics to
bridge the chasm which obviously exists in the moral and
social fabric of contemporary society' (in Centola, 1995; 125).

Later productions
There have been few major productions of *After the Fall* since
1964, but several of them are notable. In November 1964,
Franco Zeffirelli directed the European premiere by Genoa's
Teatro Stabile at the Teatro Eliseo in Rome, with Monica
Vitti as Maggie and Giorgio Albertazzi as Quentin. The
production was considered 'the event of the moment in Italy
and not only in the theatre' (*The Times*, 2 November 1964).
The review stated that the production demonstrated
Zeffirelli's deserved reputation as 'one of the great set
designers of our times', describing the set as 'a Kafkian

corridor of metallic tubes stretching to infinity', in which
there was no need to use the guard tower asked for in the
stage directions because 'this set is already a gas chamber, as
well as all the other symbols in Quentin's memory, a
courthouse, a prison ("all America's a prison"?), a suicidal
subway tunnel.' When a table or bed was needed, its shape
rose up from the patterned floor. While the set received a
great deal of attention, the performances of Albertazzi and
Vitti were also praised, and Vitti was given credit for
investing Maggie with intelligence and making 'a valiant
attempt to convince us that Maggie is not Marilyn Monroe'.
Miller thought this production 'quite marvelous' and unlike
other productions that he considered too realistic, he said
that Zeffirelli 'understood that this was a play which reflected
the world as one man saw it. Through the play the mounting
awareness of this man was the issue, and as it approached
agony the audience was to be enlarged in its consciousness of
what was happening' (quoted in O. Carlisle and R. Styron,
'The Art of the Theatre II', in Roudané, 102).

In 1982, Frank Langella bought the rights to the play,
looking towards a New York revival. This finally took place
in November 1984 at New York's Playhouse 91 in a well-
received production directed by John Tillinger, with
Langella as Quentin and Diane Wiest as Maggie. After
twenty years, the feelings about Miller's portrayal of the
figures in his life had modified enough so that the critic
Frank Rich could write, 'it's immaterial now, as ever,
whether Quentin is actually a stand-in for Mr Miller – or
whether other characters represent Marilyn Monroe, Elia
Kazan and Lee Strasberg. The real issue is what, if
anything, the playwright has created out of his past' (*New
York Times*, 5 October 1984). Samuel Freedman noted that
the casting of the 'lithe, brown-haired Miss Wiest' liberated
the play from 'one of its usual burdens – the equating of
Maggie with Marilyn Monroe' (*New York Times*, 5 November
1984). Both Wiest and Langella were critically acclaimed for
their performances and there was a much deeper
recognition of the play's meaning than there had been in
1964. As Freedman commented, 'in a drama that makes

people uncomfortable – and that is its strength as well as its weakness – they have won the applause of both critics and audiences'. Langella had consulted Miller about the play and the playwright had talked to him freely about it. The actor commented that 'Quentin is a man on a quest. I'm sure, in fact, that's why Arthur named him Quentin. And playing him is difficult in the same sense the play is difficult to take; you're asking an awful lot of yourself and the people around you to face this murderous instinct, this need to survive everything. It's the same reason this play has as many detractors as supporters' (quoted in Freedman). Although Rich complained that 'John Lee Beatty's gray, couch-laden set represents Quentin's mind as a high-tech furniture showroom', he and the play's other critics were generally appreciative of Tillinger's production. 'It's hard to imagine a better – or, for that matter, another – production of *After the Fall* for some time to come', was Rich's final judgement.

The most successful revival of *After the Fall* was probably the 1990 production by the National Theatre in London, which began with a sold-out run at the small Cottesloe Theatre before it moved to the larger Lyttelton to complete its run. Directed by Michael Blakemore, the production's most remarked-upon feature was the casting of Josette Simon, a black actress, as Maggie. Blakemore thought that casting a black actress as Maggie would not only dispel the immediate identification with Marilyn Monroe, but would also open up the character to broader implications. Thinking of Maggie's past as 'shared by some black singers who rose to fame from the mean streets of America's inner cities', Blakemore reread the play and, he said, 'it seemed quite uncannily to fit, and it also fitted in with Quentin's sort of liberal aspirations, with the kind of man who might have made that kind of bold gesture in the early 60s' (quoted in Sheila Rule, *New York Times*, 5 August 1990). When Blakemore broached the idea with Miller, he agreed with him and he expressed his hearty approval of Simon's performance during the rehearsal process.

Both Josette Simon and James Laurenson, who played

Quentin, were praised by critics, Laurenson for his 'beautifully understated performance' and Simon for completely reinterpreting the part of Maggie. In her hands, there was not only no trace of Monroe but, wrote Michael Billington, 'the part becomes an indictment of a society that arbitrarily bestows mythical fame on the unwary' (*Guardian*, 22 June 1990). Both Blakemore's direction and the set by Hayden Griffin, 'a Vorticist spiral leading to infinity that both encapsulates Quentin's tormented dreamscape and reminds you of the long shadow cast by the stone tower of the concentration camp' (ibid.), received high praise as well. In his thoughtful review, Billington noted that, 'seeing the play now at the Cottesloe, we can grasp that it is about much wider issues: survival guilt, personal responsibility, the post-Holocaust loss of innocence'.

After the Fall has been produced in regional theatres in the US with varying success. A 1987 production at the Salt City Center for the Performing Arts in Syracuse, New York, was well received, as was a 2005 production at Houston's Alley Theatre. In 1992, the playwright's daughter, Rebecca Miller, directed a production at the Ensemble Theatre in Cincinnati, commenting pointedly that the play 'doesn't have to be interpreted as autobiographical' (*Washington Times*, 25 August 1992). The most recent Broadway revival was the 2004 production by New York's not-for-profit Roundabout Theatre Company at its Broadway venue, the American Airlines Theatre. The production was directed by Michael Mayer and the set, which *Variety* described as a 'soaring version of the triumphal TWA terminal at Idlewild Airport', was designed by Richard Hoover. Both the direction and the set received mixed reviews. *Variety* reported that 'the expansive space, whose thrusting staircases and multiple platforms define it as a place of dramatic entrances and exits, plays right into Michael Mayer's hands', and that 'Mayer has a great feel for the complex construction of Miller's play, staging its fragmented scenes with a fluidity that allows characters to transcend time and place to converge in the constant present' (Marilyn Stasio, *Variety*, 2 August 2004). John Heilpern, noting that

the first line of the play is 'the action takes place in the
mind, thought, and memory of Quentin', asked whether
anyone could figure out why director and designer had
chosen 'to stage the play in an airport lounge'. 'The
playwright's stated intention is absolutely central to the
play,' he wrote. 'He wants to reproduce the interior life of a
man in crisis as certain visions and memories swirl in a near-
surreal nightmare. An airport lounge doesn't do it: It's
static, literal and earthbound' (*New York Observer*, 9 August
2004). While the reception of the direction and the design
was mixed, there was near unanimity among the critics
about the acting. All agreed that television actor Peter
Krause had been severely miscast in his Broadway debut.
Although Carla Guigino was also a television actor, her
Broadway debut performance as Maggie was much better
received than Krause's, but it was still shadowed by the
spectre of Marilyn Monroe.

Film and video
In June 1964, six months after the premiere at Lincoln
Center, the Italian producer Carlo Ponti announced that he
had bought the rights to the play for $500,000. Miller
confirmed the sale and that he was going to write the
screenplay. The intention was for Paul Newman to play
Quentin and Ponti's wife, Sophia Loren, to play Maggie.
This plan was never realised and no film version has been
made of *After the Fall*, but it was adapted for television.

In June 1973, the American television network NBC
announced plans to collaborate with the BBC on several
projects for the following season. One of these was a two-
hour production of *After the Fall* that was adapted for
television by Miller and produced and directed by Gilbert
Cates. It was first broadcast on 10 December 1974. The
actors included Christopher Plummer as Quentin, Faye
Dunaway as Maggie, Bibi Andersson as Holga, Mariclare
Costello as Louise, Murray Hamilton as Mickey and Nancy
Marchand as Quentin's Mother. In adapting the play,
Miller had to shorten it considerably and he made some

wholesale cuts, such as eliminating Felice and cutting most
of the scenes with the family, including the scene in which
the Mother has 'betrayed' the young Quentin by going off
on a trip without telling him and all of the scenes with Dan
except for the hospital scene.

The television script was more sharply focused on
Quentin's three marriages than the play, particularly on the
marriage to Maggie. The Mother's role was cut back to
focus on her betrayal of her husband rather than her
relationship with Quentin, but the viewer was constantly
reminded of her by the recurring image of her saying 'You
idiot!' or 'My bonds!' The women were presented in more
sexual terms than might have been expected from the
television of the 1970s, with Elsie (Jennifer Warren) shot
from behind to show that she was nude except for the robe
over one shoulder and Maggie walking around wrapped
loosely in a sheet. One scene showed Quentin and Maggie
in bed making love, although it was a tight two-shot of their
heads with the edges blurred.

Besides the women, Miller's script emphasised the two
historical realities of the Holocaust and the HUAC hearings.
The image of the guard tower was repeatedly introduced,
but the scene when Quentin and Holga discuss the
Holocaust was moved from the concentration camp to a
restaurant. It opens with a man, who has been talking to
Holga in German, leaving the table. She tells Quentin that
he is a professor who has asked her to help him get his book
published. When Quentin says that he seemed like a nice
man, Holga lightly says that he tried to have her killed when
she was at the university and had her sent into forced labour
because she wouldn't join the Hitler Youth. This story,
roughly based on facts from Inge Morath's life, replaced the
story of Holga's aid to her uncle, one of the Nazi officers
who tried to assassinate Hitler, that is in the play. Less
sensational, the new scene has more of the ring of truth
about it, and fits better with the character of Holga as she is
portrayed in the production, essentially as a smiling but
passive image of hope, often depicted with her arms full of
wild flowers. Three scenes are given to the HUAC issue.

The discussion with Mickey is a full scene with a fully constructed realistic set. The short scene of the hearing where Quentin is representing the minister Harley Barnes is shown briefly in a rather expressionistic style, with the committee members ranged across the screen on a high judicial bench and one of them shouting self-righteously. Lou's suicide, only alluded to in the play, is dramatised in the teleplay, with Lou on a crowded subway platform leaping to his death on the tracks.

In adapting the play to television, the theatrical techniques for dramatising the mind of Quentin had to be replaced with video techniques. Instead of the multi-layered platforms, several flat sets that represented the locales of the play were used, some places merely suggested, like the park, which consisted of a bench and a lamp post, with some fully constructed and realistically detailed sets, such as the living rooms in Quentin and Louise's apartment and country home, and Quentin and Maggie's living room and bedroom. At the beginning of the production, Plummer walked towards the camera and spoke the lines that are addressed to the Listener directly into it, giving the impression that he was addressing the audience. At the opening, an image of the various sets formed the background behind Quentin, but this was blacked out as he spoke his opening monologue. The concept of the Listener was never developed in the production, which left the dramatic framework of Quentin's quest for understanding unexpressed and the arc of the play somewhat vague. John O'Connor in the *New York Times* complained that the character said, 'Hello, good to see you again' to the audience which he has never seen before (10 December 1974).

Because the set no longer allowed all the characters to be on stage throughout the play, a solution had to be found for introducing them when they would have 'come to life' on stage. The solution was to juxtapose a small image of the character or scene next to Quentin's head, forming a sort of 'thought bubble' as in a comic strip. Thus Maggie's face appears when he first mentions her, then Holga's. The segue into the first scene, the hospital scene, was executed by having a small image of the scene appear as Quentin spoke of his father, having him turn towards it, and then cutting away from the close-up on Quentin to a full-screen shot of the hospital scene as Quentin entered it and began to interact with the characters. Before the scene with Holga, the tower from the concentration camp appeared first, next to Quentin's head, then the director cut away to Quentin sitting with Holga. This technique appears crude now, an almost humorous distraction from the flow of the drama. Viewers in the 1970s did not seem to have been particularly distracted or put off by it, however.

Towards the end of the drama, when Quentin strangles Maggie, a close-up of her face glows red and then morphs into a close-up of his mother's face, producing a startling if melodramatic version of the scene in the play. At the end, a close-up of Quentin's face is first juxtaposed with a smiling Holga saying 'Hello' and then surrounded by small images of the various sets of the play, giving some sense of the whole drama as taking place inside his mind. This technique was not nearly as effective at conveying the idea of the mindscape as the play's staging, however, and juxtaposed with the solid realism of most of the sets, the efforts at conveying the play's expressionistic elements were unfortunately more confusing than enlightening. Overall, the production was moderately successful, with Christopher Plummer and Faye Dunaway receiving praise for their acting.

Further Reading

Works by Miller

Arthur Miller Plays, 6 vols with introductions by Miller (vol. 1: *All My Sons, Death of a Salesman, The Crucible, A Memory of Two Mondays, A View from the Bridge*; vol. 2: *The Misfits, After the Fall, Incident at Vichy, The Price, Creation of the World, Playing for Time*; vol. 3: *The American Clock, The Archbishop's Ceiling, Two-Way Mirror*; vol. 4: *The Golden Years, The Man Who Had All the Luck, I Can't Remember Anything, Clara*; vol. 5: *The Last Yankee, The Ride Down Mount Morgan, Almost Everybody Wins*; vol. 6: *Broken Glass, Mr Peters' Connections, Resurrection Blues, Finishing the Picture*).
    London: Methuen Drama, 1988–2009
All My Sons, with commentary and notes by Toby Zinman.
    London: Methuen Drama, 2010
The Crucible, with commentary and notes by Susan C. W.
    Abbotson. London: Methuen Drama, 2010
Death of a Salesman, with commentary and notes by Enoch Brater.
    London: Methuen Drama, 2010
The Last Yankee, with commentary and notes by Katherine
    Egerton. London: Methuen Drama, 2011
A Memory of Two Mondays, with commentary and notes by Joshua
    Polster. London: Methuen Drama, 2011
The Price, with commentary and notes by Jane K. Dominik.
    London: Methuen Drama, 2011
A View from the Bridge, with commentary and notes by Stephen
    Marino. London: Methuen Drama, 2010
Echoes Down the Corridor: Collected Essays 1944–2000, ed. Steven R.
    Centola. London: Methuen, 2000
The Portable Arthur Miller, ed. Christopher Bigsby. New York:
    Penguin, 2003
The Theatre Essays of Arthur Miller, ed. Robert A. Martin. London:
    Methuen, 1994
Timebends: A Life. London: Methuen, 1987

Biographies

Bigsby, Christopher, *Arthur Miller: 1915–1962*. London: Weidenfeld & Nicolson, 2008

Brater, Enoch. *Arthur Miller: A Playwright's Life and Works*. London: Thames and Hudson, 2005

Gottfried, Martin. *Arthur Miller: His Life and Work*. Cambridge, MA: Da Capo, 2003

Interviews

Bigsby, Christopher, *Arthur Miller and Company*. London: Methuen, 1990

Centola, Steven R., *Arthur Miller in Conversation*. Dallas: Northouse and Northouse, 1993

Gussow, Mel, *Conversations with Miller*. New York: Applause, 2002

Roudané, Matthew, *Conversations with Arthur Miller*. Jackson: University Press of Mississippi, 1987

General critical studies

Abbotson, Susan C. W., *Critical Companion to Arthur Miller: A Literary Reference to His Life and Work*. New York: Facts on File, 2007

——, *Student Companion to Arthur Miller*. Westport, CT: Greenwood, 2000

Bigsby, Christopher, *Arthur Miller: A Critical Study*. Cambridge: Cambridge University Press, 2005

——, ed., *The Cambridge Companion to Arthur Miller*. Cambridge: Cambridge University Press, 1997

Brater, Enoch, *Arthur Miller's America: Theater & Culture in a Time of Change*. Ann Arbor: University of Michigan Press, 2005

——, ed., *Arthur Miller's Global Theater: How an American Playwright Is Performed on Stages Around the World*. Ann Arbor: University of Michigan Press, 2007

Centola, Steven R., ed., *The Achievement of Arthur Miller: New Essays*. Dallas: Contemporary Research Press, 1995

Evans, Richard I. and Robert Whitehead, *Psychology and Arthur Miller*. New York: Dutton, 1969

Griffin, Alice, *Understanding Arthur Miller*. Columbia, SC:
   University of South Carolina Press, 1996
Marino, Stephen A., *A Language Study of Arthur Miller's Plays: The
   Poetic in the Colloquial*. Lewiston, NY: Mellen, 2002
Martin, Robert A., ed., *Arthur Miller: New Perspectives*. Englewood
   Cliffs, NJ: Prentice-Hall, 1982
Mason, Jeffrey D., *Stone Tower: The Political Theater of Arthur Miller*.
   Ann Arbor: University of Michigan Press, 2008
Meyer, Nancy and Richard, '"After the Fall": A View from the
   Director's Notebook', *Annual of the Repertory Theatre of Lincoln
   Center*, ed. Barry Hyams. New York: Hill & Wang, 1965
Murphy, Brenda, *Congressional Theatre: Dramatizing McCarthyism on
   Stage, Film, and Television*. Cambridge: Cambridge University
   Press, 1999
Otten, Terry, *The Temptation of Innocence in the Dramas of Arthur
   Miller*. Columbia, MO: University of Missouri Press, 2002
Schlueter, June and James K. Flanagan, *Arthur Miller*. New York:
   Ungar, 1987

Articles on *After the Fall*

Balakian, Janet N., 'The Holocaust, the Depression, and
   McCarthyism: Miller in the Sixties', in *The Cambridge
   Companion to Arthur Miller*, ed. Christopher Bigsby, Cambridge:
   Cambridge University Press, 1997, 115–38
Centola, Steven R., 'The Monomyth and Arthur Miller's *After the
   Fall*'. *Studies in American Drama, 1945–Present* 1 (1986), 49–60
——, 'Unblessed Rage for Order: Arthur Miller's *After the Fall*'.
   *Arizona Quarterly: A Journal of American Literature, Culture, and
   Theory* 39 (Spring 1983), 62–70
Engle, John D., 'The Metaphor of Law in *After the Fall*'. *Notes on
   Contemporary Literature* 9, no. 3 (1979), 11–12
Martin, Robert A., 'Arthur Miller's *After the Fall*: "A Play about a
   Theme"'. *American Drama* 6 (Autumn 1996), 73–88
——, 'Arthur Miller's *After the Fall*: The Critical Context' in *The
   Achievement of Arthur Miller: New Essays*, ed. Steven R. Centola.
   Dallas: Contemporary Research Press, 1995, 119–26
Moss, Leonard, 'Biographical and Literary Allusion in *After the
   Fall*'. *Educational Theatre Journal* 18 (1966), 34–40

Murphy, Brenda, 'Arendt, Kristeva, and Arthur Miller:
    Forgiveness and Promise in *After the Fall*'. *PMLA: Publications of
    the Modern Language Association of America* 117 (March 2002),
    314–16

——, 'Uneasy Collaboration: Miller, Kazan, and *After the Fall*',
    Arthur Miller Journal 1 (Spring 2006), 49–59

Murray, Edward, 'Point of View in *After the Fall*'. *College Language
    Association Journal* 10 (1966), 135–42

Pagan, Nicholas O., 'Arthur Miller and the Rhetoric of Ethnic
    Self-Expression'. *Journal of American Studies* 42 (April 2008),
    89–106

Quigley, Austin E., 'Setting the Scene: *Death of a Salesman* and
    After the Fall' in *Arthur Miller's America: Theater & Culture in a
    Time of Change*, ed. Enoch Brater. Ann Arbor: University of
    Michigan Press, 2005, 60–77

Royal, Derek Parker, 'Camusian Existentialism in Arthur
    Miller's *After the Fall*'. *Modern Drama* 43 (Summer 2000),
    192–203

Stanton, Stephen S., 'Pessimism in *After the Fall*' in *Arthur Miller:
    New Perspectives*, ed. Robert A. Martin. Englewood Cliffs, NJ,
    Prentice-Hall, 1982, 159–72

Stinson, John J., 'Structure in *After the Fall*: The Relevance of the
    Maggie Episodes to the Main Themes and the Christian
    Symbolism'. *Modern Drama* 10 (1967), 233–40

Wertheim, Albert, 'Arthur Miller: *After the Fall* and After' in
    Essays on Contemporary American Drama. Munich: Hueber, 1981,
    19–32

Zeifman, Hersh, 'All My Sons After the Fall: Arthur Miller and
    the Rage for Order' in *The Theatrical Gamut: Notes for a Post-
    Beckettian Stage*, ed. Enoch Brater. Ann Arbor: University of
    Michigan Press, 1995, 107–20

After the Fall

Characters

Quentin
Felice
Dan
Mother
Elsie
Louise
Carrie
Chairman
Holga
Father
Maggie
Lou
Mickey
Lucas
Harley Barnes
Nurses, porter, secretary, hospital attendant,
a group of **boys,** *and* **passers-by**

Act One

The action takes place in the mind, thought, and memory of **Quentin**.

Except for one chair there is no furniture in the conventional sense; there are no walls or substantial boundaries.

The setting consists of three levels rising to the highest at the back, crossing in a curve from one side of the stage to the other. A stairway, center, connects them. Rising above all, and dominating the stage, is the blasted stone tower of a German concentration camp. Its wide lookout windows are like eyes which at the moment seem blind and dark; bent reinforcing rods stick out of it like broken tentacles.

On the two lower levels are sculpted areas; indeed, the whole effect is neolithic, a lava-like, supple geography in which, like pits and hollows found in lava, the scenes take place. The mind has no color but its memories are brilliant against the grayness of its landscape. When people sit they do so on any of the abutments, ledges, or crevices. A scene may start in a confined area, but spread or burst out onto the entire stage, overrunning any other area.

People appear and disappear instantaneously, as in the mind; but it is not necessary that they walk off the stage. The dialogue will make clear who is 'alive' at any moment and who is in abeyance.

The effect, therefore, will be the surging, flitting, instantaneousness of a mind questing over its own surfaces and into its depths.

The stage is dark. Now there is a sense that some figure has moved in the farthest distance; a footstep is heard, then others. As light dimly rises the persons in the play move in a random way up from beneath the high back platform. Whispering emanates from them. Some sit at once, others come farther downstage, seem to recognize one another; still others move alone and in total separateness; in short, there is a totally random congeries of movements in a slow but not dream-like rhythm. One of them, **Quentin**, *a man in his forties, moves out of this mass and down the depth of the stage to the chair. This chair faces front, toward the audience. A sharp light now isolates it. All movement ceases.* **Quentin** *reaches forward over the chair back to shake the hand of the* **Listener**, *who, if he could be seen, would be sitting just beyond the edge of the stage itself.*

Quentin   Hello! God, it's good to see you again! I'm very well.
I hope it wasn't too inconvenient on such short notice. Fine,
I just wanted to say hello, really. Thanks. (*He sits on invitation.*)
How've you been? You look sunburned . . . Oh! I've never been
to South America, you enjoy it? That's nice . . . Do I? I guess I
am, I'm quite healthy – I do a lot of walking now. (*Slight pause.*)
I started to call you a couple of times this year. Last year too . . .
Well, I lost the impulse; I wasn't sure what I wanted to say, and
at my age it's discouraging to still have to go wandering around
in one's mind. Actually, I called you on the spur of the moment
this morning; I have a bit of a decision to make. You know –
you mull around about something for months and all of a
sudden there it is and you're at a loss for what to do. Were you
able to give me two hours? It might not take that long, but I
think it involves a great deal and I'd rather not rush. Fine.

He sets himself to begin, looks off.

Ah . . .

Interrupted, he turns back to **Listener**, *surprised.*

Quentin   I've quit the firm, didn't I write you about that?
Really! I was sure I'd written . . . Oh, about fourteen months
ago; a few weeks after Maggie died . . . No, no. I've withdrawn
completely. I still hold my interest, such as it is, but I'm out of
it . . . Well, it just got to where I couldn't concentrate on a case
any more; not the way I used to. It's hard to describe; it all lost
its necessity; I was going on because I'd started out to become a
successful attorney, and I'd become one – I felt I was merely in
the service of my own success. There has to be some semblance
of a point, and I couldn't find it any more. Although I do
wonder sometimes if I am simply trying to destroy myself . . .
Well, I have walked away from what passes for an important
career . . . Not very much, I'm afraid; I still live in the hotel, see
a few people, read a good deal – (*Smiles.*) – stare out the window.
I don't know why I'm smiling; maybe I feel that's all over now,
and I'll harness myself to something again. Although I've had
that feeling before and done nothing about it, I –

Again, interrupted, he looks surprised.

God, I wrote you about *that*, didn't I? Maybe I dream these
letters . . . Mother died. Oh, it's four, five months ago, now.
Yes, quite suddenly; I was in Germany at the time and . . . it's
one of the things I wanted to talk to you about. I . . . met a
woman there. (*He grins.*) I never thought it could happen again,
but we became quite close. In fact, she's arriving tonight for
some conference at Columbia. She's an archaeologist . . . I'm
not sure, you see, if I want to lose her, and yet it's outrageous
to think of committing myself again . . . Well, yes, but look at
my life. A life, after all, is evidence, and I have two divorces in
my safe-deposit box.

He stands, moves, thinks.

I tell you frankly I'm a little afraid . . . Of who and what I'd be
bringing to her. And I thought if I could say aloud what I see
when I'm alone . . . Well, for example, this:

He sits again, leans forward.

You know . . . more and more I see that for many years I
looked at life like a case at law. It was a series of proofs. When
you're young you prove how brave you are, or smart; then,
what a good lover; then, a good father; finally, how wise, or
powerful or what-the-hell-ever. But underlying it all, I see now,
there was a presumption. That one moved not in a dry circle
but on an upward path toward some elevation, where . . . God
knows what . . . I would be justified, or even condemned. A
verdict, anyway. I think now that my disaster really began
when I looked up one day . . . and the bench was empty. No
judge in sight. And all that remained was the endless argument
with oneself, this pointless litigation of existence before an
empty bench . . . Which, of course, is another way of saying –
despair, and no great news. Some of the best, most energetic
lawyers I know believe in nothing, and even find a joy in
proving again and again that men are worthless, including
their own clients. Despair can be a way of life, providing you
believe in it. And I say to myself, pick it up, take it to heart,
and move on again. Instead, I seem to be hung up, waiting for
some . . . believable sign. And the days and the months . . .
and now the years . . . are draining away. (*Slight pause.*) A couple

of weeks ago I became aware of a strange fact. With all this darkness, the truth is that every morning when I awake, I'm full of hope! With everything I know . . . I open up my eyes . . . I'm like a boy! For an instant there's some . . . unformed promise in the air. I jump out of bed, I shave, I can't wait to finish breakfast – and then . . . it seeps in my room, the world, my life, and its pointlessness. And I thought . . . if I could corner that hope, find what it consists of, and either kill it for a lie, or really make it mine . . .

Felice *enters in sweater and skirt, sits on the floor.*

Felice   I just saw you walking by, that's all, and I thought, why don't I talk to you? You do remember me, don't you?

Quentin (*with a glance at* **Felice**)   For instance, I ran into a girl on the street last month; I'd settled her divorce a few years ago and she recognized me. And I hadn't had a woman in so long and she obviously wanted to . . .

Felice   No! I just wanted to be near you. I love your face. You have a kind face . . . You remember in your office, when my husband was refusing to sign the papers?

Quentin (*to* **Listener**)   It's this: somehow, whatever I look at, I seem to see its death.

He turns to her.

Felice   Well, see, he was always so childish alone with me; like a little stubborn boy. And when you talked to him – I could see it, he felt like a man. Like he had dignity. And me too. I felt like a grown-up woman. And I swear . . . when we walked out of your office, I . . . I almost loved him! And he asked me something when we got down in the street. Should I tell you? Or do you know already?

Quentin (*in frustration*)   I'm afraid it's pointless, I don't know why I –

Breaks off, still to **Listener***:*

Well, just that he asked her to go to bed with him, one last time . . .

Felice   How did you know that!

Quentin (*he is caught by her suddenly; his tone is answering her*)
Because it's very hard to see the death of love, and simply walk
away. (*He is now turning to face her.*)

Felice   You think I should have?

Quentin   Well, what harm would it have done?

Felice   That's what *I* wondered! Except, it would be funny,
wouldn't it? The same day we got a divorce? See, I wanted it
to mean something, the divorce!

Quentin   Honey . . . you never stop loving whoever you
loved. Hatred doesn't wipe it out.

Louise *appears, brushing her hair.* **Maggie** *sits up from the upper
platform, her breathing beginning to be heard. And* **Quentin** *becomes
active and agitated, and speaks to the* **Listener**.

Quentin   Why do I make such stupid statements? I don't
believe that! These goddamned women have injured me; have
I learned nothing?

Holga *appears beneath the tower, her arms full of flowers.*

Holga   Would you like to see Salzburg? I think they play *The
Magic Flute* tonight.

Quentin *is facing up to her. A pause. He turns back to* **Listener**.

Quentin   It's that . . . I don't know what I'd be bringing to
that girl.

Holga *is gone, and* **Maggie** *and* **Louise**.

Quentin   I don't know what I believe about my own life!
What? (*He turns to* **Felice**.) Well, death in the sense that she
was trying so damned hard to be hopeful, and I . . .

Felice   I don't deny he loved me, but . . . everything came
down to how much mileage you got on a Volkswagen! I just
wished we could get lost in some goddamn wilderness or
something, and scream and bite each other and . . . and start
going toward something!

Quentin   Well, you're in the wilderness now, aren't you? You live alone, leave the bed unmade, get a hamburger at three in the morning, sleep with who you like. You feel you're going toward something?

Felice   I think so. I feel I'm good now, as a dancer . . . or almost. I almost feel free, when I dance. Not quite, but . . . sometimes I only have to think high and I go high; I have a long thought and I fly across the floor; sometimes, sometimes I'm almost exactly what I imagine, and when that happens . . .

She has danced out of sight.

Quentin   Death in this sense: I'm sure her hope is real to her, but I sit there and see the day her legs will lose their spring, and her body will no longer follow those high leaping thoughts . . . Yes, but there's always time to die, why reach for it? In fact, she came back again the other night, almost flew into my room! And it struck me with great force – how little I really believe in life.

Felice *appears, standing, with a coat on; she is straight, nearly ecstatic.*

Felice   I had my nose fixed! Are you very busy? The doctor took the bandage off but I put it back on. I wanted you to be the first. Do you mind?

Quentin   No. But why me?

Felice   Because . . . remember that night when I came up here? I was trying to make up my mind . . . I mean there's something sort of insincere about changing your nose. I mean there could be. If that's all that makes or breaks you, the shape of a piece of cartilage? I mean if you're going to go through life building everything on *that* . . . You don't absolutely have to answer, but . . . I think you wanted to make love to me that night. Didn't you?

Quentin   I did, yes.

Felice   I knew it! And it just clicked something for me. Because you really listened to me and didn't just try to roll me over. I felt it didn't matter what kind of nose I had, so I – I might as well have a short one! Can I show it to you?

Quentin   I'd like very much to see it.

Felice   Close your eyes.

He does. She lifts the invisible bandage.

Okay.

He looks. She raises her arm in blessing.

I'll always bless you. Always!

He turns away, slowly returns to the chair as she walks into darkness.

Quentin (*to the* **Listener**)   Maybe it's this: she meant nothing to me, it was a glancing blow, and yet it's not impossible that I stand in her mind like some corner she turned in her life. I feel like a mirror in which she somehow saw herself as . . . glorious. The truth is, I even liked her first nose better!

Two pallbearers in the distance carry an invisible coffin.

It's like my mother's funeral; I still hear her voice in the street sometimes, loud and real, calling my name. She's under the ground but she's not impressively dead to me. That whole cemetery . . . I saw it like a field of buried mirrors in which people saw themselves. I don't seem to know how to grieve. Or is it just some hardness in it bothers me?

Holga *appears above, flowers in her arms.*

Quentin   God, maybe I ought to live alone; or maybe I don't believe that grief is grief unless it kills you.

Holga *is gone.* **Dan** *appears. A nurse is whispering in his ear.*

Quentin   Like when I flew back and met my brother in the hospital.

The nurse hurries out, and **Dan** *speaks to the empty air.*

Dan   I'm so glad you got here, kid; I wouldn't have wired you but I don't know what to do. You have a good flight?

Now **Father** *appears in a 'bed'. The same nurse is puffing up his pillow.*

Father   Is that my sons in the hall? Where's my wife?

Quentin (*to* **Dan**)   But what's the alternative? She's dead, he has to know.

Father   Why don't they come in? Where's my daughter?

Dan   But he was only operated on this morning. How can we walk in and say, 'Your wife is dead'? It's like sawing off his arm. Suppose we tell him she's on her way, then give him a sedative?

Quentin   But Dan, I think it belongs to him, doesn't it? After fifty years you . . . owe one another a death?

Dan (*in agony*)   Kid, the woman was his right hand. Without her he was never very much, you know. He'll fall apart.

Quentin   I can't agree; I think he can take it, he's got a lot of stuff.

Without halt, to the **Listener***:*

Which is hilarious! . . . Well, because! He was always the one who idolized the old man, and I saw through him from the beginning; suddenly we're changing places, like children in a game! I don't know what I am to anybody!

Dan (*as though he had come to a decision*)   All right; let's go in, then.

Quentin   You want me to tell him?

Dan (*unwillingly, afraid but challenged*)   I'll do it.

Quentin   I could do it, Dan.

Dan (*relieved*)   All right; if you don't mind.

They turn together toward **Father** *in the 'bed'. He does not see them yet. They move with the weight of their news.*

Quentin   It belongs to him, Dan, as much as his wedding.

He turns to the **Listener** *as he walks.*

Or is it simply that . . .

They have come to a halt near **Father***'s 'bed'.*

. . . I am crueler than he?

The nurse glances up at them and goes upstage, but waits there, apparently squinting into an upheld hypodermic needle. Now **Father** *sees them and raises up his arm.*

Father   For cryin' out loud! Look who's here! I thought you were in Europe!

Quentin   Just got back. How are you?

Dan   You look wonderful, Dad.

Father   What do you mean, 'look'? I *am* wonderful! I tell you, I'm ready to go through it again!

They laugh proudly with him.

I mean it – the way that doctor worries, I finally told him, 'Look, if it makes you feel so bad you lay down and I'll operate!' Very fine man. I thought you'd be away couple months more.

Quentin (*hesitantly*)   I decided to come back and –

Dan (*breaking in, his voice turning strange*)   Sylvia'll be right in. She's downstairs buying you something.

Father   Oh, that's nice! I tell you something, fellas – that kid is more and more like Mother. Been here every day . . . Where is Mother? I been calling the house.

The slightest empty, empty pause.

Dan   One second, Dad, I just want to –

Crazily, without evident point, he starts calling, and moving upstage toward the nurse. **Quentin** *is staring at his father.*

Dan   Nurse! Ah . . . could you call down to the gift shop and see if my sister . . .

Father   Dan! Tell her to get some ice. When Mother comes you'll all have a drink! I got a bottle of rye in the closet. (*To* **Quentin**, *as* **Dan** *comes in closer.*) I tell you, kid, I'm going to be young. I've been thinking all day since I woke up – Mother's right; just because I got old I don't have to act old. I mean we could go to Florida, we could –

Quentin   Dad.

Father   What? Is that a new suit?

Quentin   No, I've had it.

Father (*remembering – to* **Dan**, *of the nurse*)   Oh, tell her glasses, we'll need more glasses.

Dan *feels forced to turn and start out.*

Quentin   Listen, Dad.

Dan *halts, and turns back.*

Father (*totally unaware*)   Yeah?

Quentin (*he takes* **Father**'s *hand*)   Mother died.

Father's *hand grips his abdomen as though he were stabbed; his right arm rises like a policeman ordering a stop. A gasp flies out of him.*

Quentin   She had a heart attack last night on her way home.

Father   Oh, no, no, no, no.

Quentin (*grasping his hand again*)   We didn't want to tell you but –

Father   Ahhh! Ahhh, no, no, no.

Dan   There's nothing anybody could have done, Dad.

Father (*he claps his hands together*)   Oh! Oh! Oh!

Quentin (*grasping his hand again*)   Now look, Dad, you're going to be all right, you'll –

Father (*it is all turning into a deep gasping for breath; he struggles on his 'bed', half trying to get off, his head constantly turning as though he were looking for his wife*)   Oh boy. Oh boy! No, no.

Dan   Now look, Dad, you're a hell of a fella. Dad, listen –

Father   Goddamn it! I couldn't take care of myself, I knew she was working too hard!

Quentin   Dad, it's not your fault, that can happen to anyone.

Father   But she was sitting right here. She was . . . she was right here!

Now he weeps uncontrollably into his hands. **Quentin** *puts an awkward arm around him.*

Quentin   Pa . . . Pa . . .

Now **Quentin** *grips him with both arms.* **Dan** *moves in close as though to share him. He lays a hand on* **Father***'s shoulder.*

Father   Oh, boys – she was my right hand! (*He raises his fist and seems about to lose his control again.*)

Dan   We'll take care of you, Dad. I don't want you to worry about –

Father   No – no. It's . . . I'll be all right. I'll . . . God! . . . Now I'm better! Now, *now* I'm better!

They are silent; he keeps shaking his head.

So where is she?

Quentin   In the funeral parlor.

Father (*shaking his head – an explosive blow of air*)   Paaaaaah!

Quentin   We didn't want to tell you but we figured you'd rather know.

Father   Ya. (*Pats* **Quentin***'s hand.*) Thanks. Thanks. I'll . . . (*He looks up at* **Quentin**.) I'll just have to be stronger.

Quentin   That's right, Dad.

Father (*to no one*)   This . . . will make me stronger. (*But the weeping threatens; he clenches his jaws, shakes his head, and indicates a point.*) She was right here!

Lights go out on him and **Dan**. **Quentin** *comes slowly to the* **Listener**.

Quentin   Yes, I'm proud I didn't kid him, it bothers me. I don't know, maybe that he took it so for granted I was also devastated . . . This? I hadn't thought of this as grief. I hope it is.

The tower gradually begins to light.

Still, a couple months later he bothered to register and vote . . . Well, I mean . . . it didn't kill him either, with all his tears. I don't know what the hell I'm driving at! (*He is caught by the bright tower.*) I don't get the connection at the moment but . . . I visited a concentration camp in Germany . . .

He has started toward the tower when **Felice** *appears, raising her arm in blessing.*

Felice   Close your eyes, okay?

Quentin (*turned by her force*)   I don't understand why that girl sticks in my mind . . . Yes!

He moves toward her now.

She did; she offered me some . . . love, I guess. And if I don't return it . . . or if it doesn't change me somehow, it . . . it's like owing for a gift you didn't ask for.

Felice   I'll always bless you!

Her arm raised, she walks into darkness.

Quentin   When she left, I did a stupid thing. I don't understand it. There are two light fixtures on the wall of my hotel room. (*Against his own disgust.*) I noticed for the first time that they're . . . a curious distance apart. And I suddenly saw that if you stood between them – (*He spreads out his arms.*) – you could reach out and rest your . . .

Just before he completely spreads his arms **Maggie** *sits up; her breathing sounds. He drops his arms, aborting the image.* **Maggie** *goes dark.*

Quentin   Maybe I can get to it later. I can't now . . .

Now **Holga** *appears and is bending to read the legend fixed to the wall of a torture chamber.*

Quentin   Yes, with this woman . . . Holga. She took me there.

Holga (*turning to 'him'*)   It's a general description. No, I don't mind, I'll translate it.

She returns to the legend; he slowly approaches behind her.

'In this camp a minimum of two hundred thousand Dutch, Belgian, Russian, Polish, French, and Danish prisoners of war were killed. Also, four thousand two hundred and seven refugees from the Spanish Republican Army. The door to the left leads into the chamber where their teeth were extracted for gold; the drain in the floor carried off the blood. At times instead of shooting, they were individually strangled to death. The barracks on the right were the bordello where women prisoners were forced to – '

Quentin (*touching her shoulder*)   I think you've had enough, Holga.

Holga   No, if you want to see the rest . . . (*She bursts into tears, but in silence, and quickly turns away.*) Come, I don't mind.

Quentin (*taking her arm*)   Let's walk, dear. Country looks lovely out there.

They walk. The light changes to day.

Here, this grass looks dry; let's sit down.

They sit. Pause.

I always thought the Danube was blue.

Holga   Only the waltz. Although it does change near Vienna. Out of some lingering respect for Strauss, I suppose.

Quentin   I don't know why this hit me so; I suddenly got a cracking headache in there.

Holga   I'm sorry. It's just that you seemed so interested in the Nazi period, and we were passing so close . . .

Quentin   No, I'm glad I saw it.

Holga (*starting to rise; she senses an estrangement*)   I have some aspirin in the car.

Quentin (*lightly touching her*)   We'll go soon. I just want to . . . sit for a minute.

Holga (*to raise his spirits*)   You still want to see Salzburg?

Quentin   Oh, sure.

Holga   I'd love to show you Mozart's house. And the cafés are excellent there.

Quentin (*turning to her now*)   Was there somebody you knew died here?

Holga   Oh, no. I feel people ought to see it, that's all. No one comes here any more. I've brought foreign colleagues once or twice.

Quentin   But why do you come back? It seems to tear you apart.

Holga   I suppose . . . one doesn't want to lose the past, even if it's dreadful. You're the first person I've met in a very long time who wants to talk about it.

Quentin   Yes, but I'm an American.

Holga   Oh, Americans too. In fact, when I first visited America after the war I was three days under questioning before they let me in. It was impossible to explain to them. How could one be in forced labor for two years if one were not a Communist? And of course, not being Jewish either, it was very suspicious. I was ready to turn back. I was so frightened. In fact, it was only when I told them I had blood relatives in several Nazi ministries that they were reassured. You see? Here it's not talked about, and outside it's not understood. It's as though fifteen years of one's life had simply vanished in some insane confusion. So I was very glad you were so interested.

Quentin (*glancing up at the tower*)   I guess I thought I'd be indignant, or angry. But it's like swallowing a lump of earth. It's strange.

He starts to cover his eyes and she presses him to lie down, and speaks cheerfully . . .

Holga   Come, lie down here for a while and perhaps –

Quentin   No, I'm – (*He has fended off her hand.*) I'm sorry, dear, I didn't mean to push you away.

Holga (*rebuffed and embarrassed*)   I see wildflowers on that hill; I'll pick some for the car!

She gets up quickly.

Quentin   Holga?

She continues off. He jumps up and hurries to her, turning her.

Holga.

He does not know what to say.

Holga (*holding back tears*)   Perhaps we've been together too much. I could rent another car at Linz; perhaps we could meet in Vienna sometime.

Quentin   I don't want to lose you, Holga.

Holga   I understand that you're leaving soon. I never expected any . . .

Quentin   But you do expect something, everybody does. You're not a woman to go to bed just for the ride.

Holga   No, I'm not. But I have settled since several years to live for my work. I am not helpless alone. It's simply that from the moment you spoke to me I felt somehow familiar, and it was never so before . . . It isn't a question of getting married; I am not ashamed this way. But I must have *something*.

Quentin   I don't give you anything? Tell me; because I've been told that before, but never so calmly.

Holga   You give me very much . . . It's difficult for me to speak like this – I am not a woman who must be reassured every minute, those women are stupid to me.

Quentin   We're good friends, Holga; say it to me.

Holga   You have nothing; but perhaps that's all you want. I can understand that after what you've lived.

Quentin   That's not it, Holga; there's nothing as dull as adventure. I've had all I can use.

Holga   But perhaps that's all there is for you.

Quentin (*he turns her face to him*)   Holga. Are you weeping . . . for *me*?

Holga   Yes.

Quentin (*struck*)   Don't go away; not yet. Will you?

Holga   I hear your wings opening, Quentin.

Quentin   I don't want to abuse your feeling for me, you understand? The truth is – and I couldn't say this if I didn't trust you – I swear I don't know if I have lived in good faith. And the doubt ties my tongue when I think of promising anything again.

Holga   But how can one ever be sure of one's good faith?

Quentin (*surprised*)   God, it's wonderful to hear you say that. All my women have been so goddamned sure!

Holga   But how can one ever be?

Quentin (*he kisses her gratefully*)   Why do you keep coming back to this place?

Pause. **Holga** *is disturbed, uncertain.*

Holga   I . . . don't know. Perhaps . . . because I didn't die here.

Quentin (*turns quickly to* **Listener**)   What?

Holga   Although that would make no sense! I don't really know!

Quentin (*goes to the chair*)   That people . . . what? 'Wish to die for the dead'? No, no, I can understand it; survival can be hard to bear. But I . . . I don't think I feel that way . . .

Maggie *again appears in bed on the upper level; she begins to heave for breath. Her face is still indistinguishable. Instantly* **Quentin** *turns away as from an opposite side of the stage a piano is heard and a woman,* **Mother**, *is in mid-song with a romantic ballad from a musical of the twenties.*

Quentin   Although I do think of my mother now, and she's dead. Yes!

He turns to **Holga**.

Quentin   Maybe the dead do bother her.

Holga   It was the middle of the war. I had just come out of a class and there were leaflets on the sidewalk. A photograph of a concentration camp. And emaciated people. It was dropped there by British Intelligence; one tended to believe the British. I had had no idea. Truly. Any more, perhaps, than Americans know how a Negro lives. I was seventeen; I lived in my studies; I planned how to cut my hair differently. It is much more complicated than it seems later. There were many officers in my family. It was our country. It isn't easy to turn against your country; not in a war. There are always reasons – do Americans turn against America because of Hiroshima? No, there are reasons always.

Pause.

And I took the leaflet to my godfather – he was still commanding our Intelligence. And I asked if it were true. 'Of course,' he said, 'why does it excite you?' And I said, 'You are a swine. You are all swine.' I threw my briefcase at him. And he opened it and put some papers in and asked me to deliver it to a certain address. And I became a courier for the officers who were planning to assassinate Hitler . . . They were all hanged.

Quentin   Why not you?

Holga   They didn't betray me.

Quentin   Then why do you say good faith is never sure?

Holga (*after a pause*)   It was my country . . . longer perhaps than it should have been. But I didn't know. And now I don't know how I could not have known. I can't imagine not knowing, now.

Quentin   Holga . . . I bless your uncertainty. Maybe that's why you're so wonderful to be with. You don't seem to be looking for some goddamned . . . moral *victory*. Forgive me, I didn't mean to be distant with you. I – (*Looks up at the tower.*) – think this place frightens me! And how is that possible? All empty!

Holga   I'll get the flowers. And maybe we can buy some cheese and apples and eat while we drive!

She starts away.

Quentin   And you forgive me?

Holga (*turns, and with great love*)   Yes! I'll be right back! And we'll go right away!

She hurries away.

Quentin *stands in stillness a moment; the presence of the tower bores in on him; its color changes; he now looks up at it and addresses the* **Listener**.

Quentin   But it's empty now! In fact, the view from here is rather pastoral; and the stone walls are warm in the sun, and quiet. I think . . . I may have imagined it more monstrous. Or bizarre. I helped a mason years ago before I went to college – I see the problem building such high walls in sandy soil . . . how dare one think of that? I think of the footings – they must go ten feet down. At least ten! I know footings! But I never thought the stones would look so ordinary.

Now he turns out.

Why do I *know* something here? Even hollow now and empty, it has a face; and asks a sort of question: 'What do you believe . . . as true as this?' Yes! Believers built this, maybe that's the fright – and I, without belief, stand here disarmed. I can see the convoys grinding up this hill; and I inside; no one knows my name and yet they'll smash my head on a concrete floor! And no appeal.

He turns quickly to the **Listener**.

Quentin   Yes! It's that I no longer see some last appeal, and here there was none either! Socialism once, then love; some final hope is gone that always saved before the end!

Mother *appears; at the same time her coffin appears above.*

Mother   Not too much cake, darling, there'll be a lot of food at this wedding. (*Calling upstage.*) Fanny? Cut him a small piece . . . well, not *that* small!

Quentin   Mother! That's strange. And murder. Or is it her comfort brings her to me in this place?

Mother   Fanny? Not too hot ironing my husband's dress shirt! (*Turns suddenly to an invisible boy.*) You are going to wear garters tonight, Quentin, and don't argue with me . . . Because it's my brother's wedding and your stockings are not to hang over your shoes!

Quentin (*he has started to laugh but it turns into*)   Why can't I mourn her? And Holga wept in there . . . why can't I weep? Why do I feel an understanding with this slaughterhouse?

Now **Felice** *appears, raising her arm.*

Quentin   I don't understand what I'm supposed to be to anyone!

Felice *is gone.* **Mother** *laughs. He turns to her, addressing the* **Listener**.

Quentin   I don't know, some wedding in the family. I don't get it.

Mother (*her laughter turning bitter*)   God! Why must every wedding in this family be a catastrophe! . . . Because the girl is pregnant, darling, and she's got no money, she's stupid, and I tell you this one is going to end up with a mustache! Five beautiful men like that and one after the other . . . I don't know where they *find* such women!

Quentin (*watching her, seated*)   But what the hell has this to do with a concentration camp?

Mother   And wants a tight gown! As though she's fooling somebody! That's why, darling, when you grow up, I hope you learn how to disappoint people. Especially women. Never forget it, dear, you're a man, and a man has all the choices. Will you stop playing with matches? (*Slaps an invisible boy's hand.*) You'll pee in bed! Why don't you practice your penmanship instead? You write like a monkey, darling.

Quentin (*shaking his head, glancing up at the tower*)   I don't get it.

Father *suddenly appears, holding an invisible phone to his ear.*

Quentin *instantly stands.*

Mother   And where is your father? If he went to sleep in a Turkish bath again, I'll . . .

Quentin *is moving toward* **Father** *as though wanting to hear what he is saying in phone; he is making a shushing gesture to* **Mother**.

Mother   What are you talking about, I didn't end up calling all the Turkish baths the night my brother Herbert got married? Forgot all about it . . . and nothing bothers him!

She laughs warmly. **Quentin** *has arrived at* **Father**, *peers at his profile.*

Father   Herman? Cable Hamburg.

Mother   Like the night of the Dempsey–Tunney fight.

Quentin   Ssh!

He turns back, eager to hear what **Father** *is saying.*

Mother   . . . The men's-room door gets stuck so by the time he gets out there's a new champion. Cost him a hundred dollars to go to the men's room!

Father   No, sixty thousand tons; sixty; Vera Cruz, the *Bismarck*'s due.

Mother   But you mustn't laugh at him, he's a wonderful man, it's just that sometimes he can drive you out of your mind.

Father   Then cable Southampton, turn him back to Finland Monday. ATO.

Mother   My wedding? Oh, no dear, my wedding . . . there was happiness.

Quentin *turns to her.*

Mother   Well, look at your father; to this day he walks into a room you want to bow! Not like my sisters, one after the other running into the house, 'Mama, I'm in love!' And with what? With who? I wasn't allowed to *see* your father till his father and Grandpa had agreed! . . . *Because,* I decided for once somebody was not going to break my mother's heart . . . What are you talking about, of course I loved him! (*Warmly.*) He'd take me to a restaurant – one look at him and the waiters started moving tables around; if he saw a thick water glass he'd walk out; there could be a line around the block to a Broadway show, he'd go right up to the box office and they'd find two tickets. *Because* dear – people know that this is a *man*. Even Doctor Strauss, at my wedding he came over to me says, 'Rose, I can see it looking at him, you've got a wonderful man,' and he was always in love with me, Strauss . . . Oh, sure, but he was only a medical student then, didn't have a penny, my father wouldn't let him in the house. Who knew he'd end up so big in gallstones? That poor boy – used to bring me novels to read, poetry, philosophy, God knows what! One time we even sneaked off to hear Rachmaninoff together . . .

She laughs sadly; with wonder more than bitterness.

That's why, you see, two weeks after we were married, sit down to dinner and Papa hands me a menu, and asks me to read it to him . . . Couldn't *read*! I got so frightened I nearly ran away! . . . 'Why'? Because your grandmother is such a fine, unselfish woman; two months in school and they put him into the shop! That's what some women are, my dear . . . and now he goes and buys her a new Packard every year and two more for his brothers! Damned fool, I could kill him! And what are we paying a chauffeur for, I can't find him half the time anyway! . . . Because if they're going to have chauffeurs I'm going to have a chauffeur – it's all our money anyway!

With a strange and deep fear.

Please, darling, I want you to *draw* the letters, that scribbling is ugly, dear; and your posture, your speech, it can all be beautiful! Ask Miss Fisher, for years they kept my handwriting pinned up on the bulletin board; they made up a special new prize to give me on graduating day. God, I'll never forget it, valedictorian of the class, with a scholarship to Hunter in my hand – (*A blackness flows into her soul.*) – and I come home, and Grandpa says, 'You're getting married!' It had never come into my mind! I was like . . . like with small wings, just getting ready to fly; I slept all year with the catalogue under my pillow. To learn, to learn everything! Oh, darling, the whole thing is such a mystery!

Father *enters the area, talking to the young, invisible* **Quentin**.

Father Quentin, would you get me the office on the phone? (*To* **Mother** *as he kisses her lightly* on *the cheek*.) Why would you call the Turkish bath?

Mother I thought you forgot about the wedding.

Father I wish I could but I'm paying for it.

Mother He'll pay you back!

Father I believe it, I just wouldn't want to hang by my hair that long.

He turns, goes to an invisible phone, stands.

Herman? Hold the wire. (*To* **Mother**.) Why don't you both go up and get dressed?

Mother (*moving up the stairs*)   I don't want to be late, now.

Father   There's time; she won't give birth if we're a half-hour late.

Mother   Don't be so smart! He fell in love, what's so terrible about that?

Father   They all fall in love on my money. Only I can't fall in love unless I pay for it. I married into a love nest! (*He turns to the invisible* **Quentin**, *warmly smiling.*) Did they pass a law that kid can't get a haircut? (*Reaching into his pocket, tossing a coin.*) Here, at least get a shine. (*To* **Mother**.) I'll be right up, dear, go ahead, get dressed. (*On phone.*) Herman? The accountant still there? Put him on.

Quentin (*suddenly, recalling*)   Oh, yes!

Mother   I'll put in your studs. God, he's so beautiful in a tuxedo!

She goes a distance out of the area but halts on the stair, turns, eavesdrops.

Father   Billy? You finished? Well what's the story, where am I?

Quentin *now turns up toward* **Mother** *on the stairs.*

Quentin   . . . Yes!

Father   Don't you read the papers? What'll I do with Irving Trust, I can't give it away. What bank?

Mother *descends a step, alarmed.*

Father   I been to every bank in New York, I can't get a bill paid, how the hell they going to lend me money? No-no, there's no money in London, there's no money in Hamburg, there ain't a cargo moving in the world, the ocean's empty, Billy . . . Now tell me the truth, where am I?

Pause. **Mother** *descends another step.* **Quentin** *is below, watching her. Now* **Mother** *descends into the area.* **Father** *stands almost stiffly, as though to take a storm.*

Mother   What's that about? What are you 'winding up'?

Father *stands staring; he speaks unheard, but she seems to have heard an additional shocking fact, then another, and another.*

Mother   What are you talking about? When did this start? . . . Well, how much are you taking out of it? . . . You lost your mind? You've got over four hundred thousand dollars' worth of stocks, you can sell the . . . You sold those wonderful stocks! When? . . . Eight months! I just bought a new grand piano, why didn't you say something? And a silver service for my brother, and you don't say anything? . . . (*More subdued, walks a few steps in thought.*) Well then, you'd better cash your insurance; you've got at least seventy-five thousand cash value . . . (*Halts, turning in shock.*) When? (**Father** *is gradually losing his stance, his grandeur; he pulls his tie loose.*) All right, then – we'll get rid of my bonds. Do it tomorrow . . . What do you mean? Well you get them back. I've got ninety-one thousand dollars in bonds you gave me. Those are my bonds. I've got bonds . . . (*Breaks off; open horror on her face and now a growing contempt.*) You mean you saw everything going down and you throw good money after bad? Are you some kind of a moron?

Father   You don't walk away from a business; I came to this country with a tag around my neck like a package in the bottom of the boat!

Mother   I should have run the day I met you!

Father (*as though stabbed*)   Rose!

He sits, closing his eyes, his neck bent.

Mother   I should have done what my sisters did, tell my parents to go to hell and thought of myself for once! I should have run for my life.

Father   Sssh, I hear the kids.

A sharp shaft of light opens a few yards away and he glances toward it.

Mother   I ought to get a divorce!

Father   Rose, the college men are jumping out of windows!

Mother But your last dollar? (*Bending over, into his face.*) You are an idiot!

Her nearness forces him to stand; they look at each other, strangers.

Quentin (*he looks up at the tower*)   Yes! For no reason – they don't even ask your name!

Father (*he looks toward the column of light*)   Somebody crying? Quentin's in there. You better talk to him.

Quentin *walks upstage, away from the light. She goes in some trepidation toward it. A foot or so from it she halts.*

Mother Darling? You better get dressed. Don't cry, dear, it'll be all right. He'll come back bigger than ever!

*She is stopped short by something '**Quentin**' has said.*

Mother What *I* said? Why, what did I say? . . . Are you crazy? I'd never say a thing like that, I thought you were upstairs. Well I was a little angry, that's all, but I never said *that*. I think he's a wonderful man! (*Laughs.*) How could I say a thing like that? Quentin!

The light rapidly fades, and as though he is disappearing she extends her arms toward the fading light.

But I didn't say anything!

With a cry toward someone lost.

Darling, I didn't say anything!

*Instantly **Holga** appears beneath the tower, with flowers in her arms. She looks about for him.*

Holga Quentin? Quentin?

*He is still staring at **Mother**, from whom he turns toward **Holga**.*

*Now **Holga** sees him and comes down to him.*

Holga Look! The car will be all sweet inside!

Quentin (*he absently sniffs the flowers, staring at her*)   You love me, don't you?

Holga   Yes.

Quentin (*glancing up at the tower*)   Do you ever feel when you come here some vague . . . complicity?

Holga   Quentin . . . no one they didn't kill can be innocent again.

Quentin (*slight pause*)   Then how do you get so purposeful, Holga? You work so hard, you seem so full of joy and hope.

Holga   While I was getting the flowers just now I thought I ought to tell you something. In a bombing once I lost my memory, and wandered everywhere with crowds across the countryside looking for a safe place. Every day, one turned away from people dying on the roads. Until one night I tried to jump from the railing of a bridge. An old soldier pulled me back and slapped my face and made me follow him; he'd lost a leg at Stalingrad, was furious that I would kill myself; I walked behind his crutches over Germany looking for some sign of who I'd been. And suddenly there was a door with a tremendous lion's-head brass knocker; I ran; I knocked; my mother opened it. My life came back! And I turned to ask the soldier in; to thank him; to feed him; to give him everything I had! But he was gone. I've been told that I imagined him, but even now at times I turn a corner and expect to find him. If we could even . . . nod to one another! I know how terrible it is to owe what one can never pay. And for a long time after I had the same dream each night – that I had a child; and even in the dream I saw that the child was my life; and it was an idiot. And I wept, and a hundred times I ran away, but each time I came back it had the same dreadful face. Until I thought, if I could kiss it, whatever in it was my own, perhaps I could rest. And I bent to its broken face, and it was horrible . . . but I kissed it.

Quentin   Does it still come back?

Holga   At times. But it somehow has the virtue now . . . of being mine. I think one must finally take one's life in one's arms, Quentin.

She takes his hand.

Come, I think they play *The Magic Flute* tomorrow. You like *The Magic Flute*?

Quentin (*he kisses her*)   One thing about you, you tell the goddamned funniest stories!

Holga (*hits him and mock-pouts*)   You're making fun of me!

Quentin   Let's get out of this dump, and . . . where we going?

Holga (*laughing*)   Salzburg!

Quentin   I'll race you to the car, last one there's a rotten egg. Or do you say a rancid wurst?

Holga (*laughing*)   Okay, I'm racing!

She gets set.

Quentin   Go!

They start running, but while she goes off into darkness **Quentin** *comes down to the chair.*

I miss her badly. And yet, I can't sign my letters to her 'With love'. I put 'Sincerely' or 'As ever', some such brilliant evasion. I've lost the sense of some absolute necessity, I think. Living alone does that; I walk down the street, I see the millions of apartment windows lighting up – I swear I don't understand how each man knows which door to go to. Can they all be in love? Is that what sorts them out? I don't think so; it's some kind of innocence, a deep belief that all their destinations are ordained. With me, whether I open a book or think of marrying again, it's so damned clear I've chosen what I do – it cuts the strings between my hands and heaven. It sounds foolish, but I feel . . . unblessed. And I look back at when there seemed to be a kind of plan, some duty in the sky. I had a dinner table, and a wife, a child, and the world so wonderfully threatened by injustices I was born to correct! How fine! Remember? When there were good people and bad people? And how easy it was to tell! The worst son of a bitch, if he loved Jews and Negroes and hated Hitler – he was a buddy. Like some kind of paradise compared to this . . . Until I begin to look at it.

Elsie *appears, a beach robe hanging from her shoulders, her arms out of the sleeves, her back to us; she is fixing her wet hair in an invisible mirror.*

Quentin   God, when I think of what I believed, I want to hide!

He stands, moves toward her.

. . . Yes, but I wasn't all that young! You would think a man of thirty-two would know that when a guest, changing out of a wet bathing suit in his bedroom . . .

Elsie, *as he approaches, turns to him, and her robe slips off one shoulder.*

Quentin   . . . and just stands there with her two bare faces hanging out . . .

Elsie   Oh, are you through working? Why don't you swim now! The water's just right.

Quentin (*with a laugh of great pain, crying out*)   I tell you I believed she didn't know she was naked! It's Eden! . . . Well, she was *married*! How could a woman who can tell when the Budapest String Quartet is playing off key, who refuses to wear silk stockings because the Japanese have invaded Manchuria, whose husband – my friend, a saintly professor of law – is editing my first appeal to the Supreme Court on the grass outside that window – I could see the top of his head past her tit, for God's sake! . . . Of course I understood, but it's what you allow yourself to admit! To admit what you see endangers principles!

Elsie *leaves the 'room' and crosses to where* **Louise** *sits.* **Quentin** *turns to them. They are talking in an intense whisper. He now approaches them from behind, halts, turns to the* **Listener**.

Quentin   You know! When two women are whispering, and they stop abruptly when you appear . . .

Elsie *and* **Louise** (*turning to him after an abrupt stop to their talking*) Hi.

In the background **Lou** *appears, reading a brief – a tender, kindly man, in shorts.*

Quentin   . . . the subject must have been sex. And if one of them is your wife . . . she must have been talking about you.

Elsie (*as though to get him to go*)   Lou's behind the house, reading your brief. He says it's superb!

Quentin   I hope so. I've been kind of nervous about what he'd say.

Elsie   I wish you'd tell him that, Quentin! Will you? Just how much his opinion means to you. It's important you tell him.

Quentin   I'll be glad to. (*Awkwardly glancing from* **Louise** *back to her.*) Nice here, isn't it?

Elsie   It's enchanting. (*Taking in* **Louise**.) I envy you both so much!

Quentin   See you. Glad you could come.

Elsie (*gets up, goes past* **Lou**)   I want one more walk before the train, dear. Did you comb your hair today?

Lou (*closing the brief*)   I think so. Quentin! This is superb! It's hardly like a brief at all; there's a majestic quality, like a classic opinion! (*Chuckling, tugs* **Quentin**'s *sleeve.*) I almost feel honored to have known you!

Elsie *is gone.*

Quentin   I'm so glad, Lou – your opinion means . . .

Lou   Your whole career will change with this, Quentin. But do me a favor, will you?

Quentin   Oh, anything, Lou.

Lou   Would you offer it to Elsie to read? I know it seems an extraordinary request, but . . .

Quentin   No, I'd be delighted!

Lou (*secretively*)   It's shaken her terribly, my being subpoenaed and all those damned headlines. Despite everything, it does affect one's whole relationship. So any gesture of respect becomes terrifically important. For example, I gave her the manuscript of my new text to read, and I've even called off publication for a while to incorporate her criticisms. It may be her psychoanalysis, but she's become remarkably acute.

Quentin   But I hope you don't delay any more, Lou; it'd be wonderful if you published something now. Just to show those bastards.

Lou   Yes . . .

Glancing toward the women, he takes **Quentin**'s *arm and strolls with him.*

Lou   I've been thinking of calling you about that, Quentin. You see, it's a textbook for the schools, and Elsie feels that it will only start a new attack on me.

Quentin   But they've investigated you, what more damage could they do?

Lou   Who knows? Another attack might knock me off the faculty. It's only Mickey's vote that saved me the last time.

Quentin   Really! I didn't know that.

Lou   Oh, yes, he made a marvelous speech at the Dean's meeting when I refused to testify.

Quentin   Well, that's Mickey.

Lou   Yes, but Elsie feels . . . I'd just be drawing down the lightning again to publish now. She even feels it's some unconscious wish for self-destruction on my part. And yet, if I put the book away, it's like a kind of suicide to me. Everything I know is in that book . . . What's your opinion?

Quentin   Lou, you have a right to publish; a radical past is not leprosy. We only turned Left because it seemed the truth was there. You mustn't be ashamed.

Lou (*in pain*)   Goddamn it, yes! Except . . . I never told you this, Quentin . . .

Quentin (*comes down to the* **Listener**)   What am I going into this for? (*Listens.*) Yes – in a way it was – the day the world ended, it all fell down, and nobody was innocent again. And yet, we never were! What am I looking for?

Lou   When I returned from Russia and published my study of Soviet law – (*Breaks off.*) I left out many things I saw. I . . . lied. For a good cause, I thought, but all that lasts is the lie. It's so strange to me now – I have many failings, but I have never been a liar. And I lied for the Party. Over and over, year after year. And that's why, now . . . with this book of mine, I want to be true to myself. You see, it's no attack I fear, but being forced to defend my own incredible lies.

Elsie *appears, approaching, hearing.*

Elsie   Lou, I'm quite surprised. I thought we'd settled this.

Lou   Yes, dear, I only wanted Quentin's feeling . . .

Elsie   Your shirt's out, dear. (*He quickly tucks it into his shorts. And to* **Quentin**.) You certainly don't think he ought to publish.

Quentin   But the alternative seems –

Elsie (*with a volcanic, suppressed alarm*)   But, dear, that's the *situation*! Lou's not like you, Quentin; you and Mickey can function in the rough and tumble of private practice, but Lou's a purely academic person. He's *incapable* of going out and . . .

Lou (*with a difficult grin and chuckle*)   Well, dear, I'm not all that delicate, I –

Elsie (*a sudden flash of contempt; to* **Lou**)   This is hardly the time for illusions!

With a smash of light **Mother** *appears, and* **Father** *slumped in a chair beside her.*

Mother   You *idiot*!

Quentin *is shocked, turns quickly to* **Mother**.

Mother   My *bonds*?

She and **Father** *are gone. Instantly, as before,* **Holga** *appears under the tower, flowers in her hand, looking about for him.*

Holga   Quentin?

He quickly turns his head toward her. She is gone.

Quentin (*alone*)   How do you believe again?

Felice *appears.*

Felice   I'll always bless you!

She turns and walks into the dark. The wall appears with the two light fixtures.

Quentin   The other night, when that girl left . . . I . . .

Turns to the wall. The fixtures light up. But he turns away, agonized.

I'll try to get to it . . .

Elsie   Come, dear, you haven't even swum. Let's enjoy this weekend!

She walks off with **Lou**, *kissing his cheek.*

Quentin (*watching them go*)   Then why does something seem to fall apart? Was it ever whole?

Louise *now stands up from the beach chair. She turns, addresses an empty space.*

Louise   Quentin?

Quentin (*he turns his eyes to the ground, then speaks to the* **Listener**)   Wasn't that a terrifying thing, what Holga said?

Louise   I've decided to go into psychoanalysis.

Quentin (*still to the* **Listener**)   To take up your life, like an idiot child?

Louise   I want to talk about some things with you.

Quentin   But can anybody really do that?

*He turns toward **Louise** now guiltily.*

Quentin   Kiss his life?

Louise (*as though he had not answered – speaking toward the empty space*)   Quentin?

He is drawn to the spot she is concentrating her gaze on. Tension rises in him as he arrives in her line of sight and faces her.

You don't have to pick up Betty now, she enjoys playing there. (*Steeling her shy self.*) I've got to make a decision.

Quentin   About what?

Louise (*in fear*)   About everything.

Quentin   What do you mean?

Louise (*at a loss for an instant*)   Sit down, will you?

*She sits, gathering her thoughts. He hesitates, as though pained at the memory, and also because at the time he lived this it was an agony. And as he approaches his chair he speaks to the **Listener**.*

Quentin   It was like . . . a meeting. In seven years we had never had a meeting. Never, never what you'd call . . . a meeting.

Louise   We don't seem . . .

A long pause while she peers at a forming thought.

. . . married.

Quentin   We?

Louise (*it is sincere, what she says, but she has had to learn the words, so there is the faintest air of a formula in her way of speaking*)   You don't pay any attention to me.

Quentin (*puzzled*)   When?

Louise   You never did. But I never realized it till . . . recently.

Quentin (*to help her*)   You mean like Friday night? When I didn't open the car door for you?

Louise   Well, that's a small thing, but it's part of what I mean, yes.

Quentin   But I told you; you always opened the car door for yourself.

Louise   I've always done everything for myself, but that doesn't mean it's right. Everybody notices it, Quentin.

Quentin   What?

Louise   The way you behave toward me. I don't . . . *exist*. People are supposed to find out about each other. I am not all this uninteresting, Quentin. Many people, men *and* women, think I *am* interesting.

Quentin   Well, I – (*Breaks off.*) I – (*Breaks off.*) I . . . don't know what you mean.

Louise   I know you don't. You have no conception of what a woman is. You think I'm some sort of . . . I don't know what I am to you.

Quentin   But I do pay attention – just last night I read you my whole brief.

Louise   Quentin, you think reading a brief to a woman is talking to her?

Quentin   But that's what's on my mind.

Louise   But if that's all on your mind what do you need a wife for?

Quentin   Now what kind of a question is that?

Louise   Quentin, that's the question!

Quentin   (*slight pause; with fear, astonishment*)   What's the question?

Louise   What am I to you? Do you . . . do you ever *ask* me anything? Anything personal?

Quentin   (*with rising alarm*)   But Louise, what am I supposed to ask you? I *know* you!

Louise   No.

She stands with dangerous dignity.

You don't know me.

Pause. She proceeds now with caution.

I don't intend to be ashamed of myself any more, I used to think it was normal; or even that you don't see me because I'm not worth seeing. But I think now that you don't really see any woman. Except in some ways your mother. You do sense her feelings; you do know when she's unhappy or anxious, but not me. Or any other woman.

Elsie *appears, about to drop her robe.*

Quentin   That's not true, though. I . . .

Louise   Elsie's noticed it too.

Quentin (*guiltily snapping away from the vision of* **Elsie**)   What?

Louise   She's amazed at you.

Quentin   Why, what'd she say?

Louise   You don't seem to . . . register the fact that a woman is *present*.

Quentin   Oh. (*He is disarmed, confused, and silent.*)

Louise   And you know how she admires you.

Quentin *nods seriously. Suddenly he turns out the* **Listener** *and bursts into an agonized, ironical laughter. He abruptly breaks it off, and returns to silence before* **Louise**.

Louise *speaks with uncertainty; it is her first attempt at confrontation.*

Louise   Quentin?

He stands in silence.

Quentin?

He is silent.

Silence is not going to solve it any more. I can't live this way. Quentin?

Quentin (*pause; he gathers courage*)   Maybe I don't speak because the one time I did tell you my feelings you didn't get over it for six months.

Louise (*angered*)   It wasn't six months, it was a few weeks. I did overreact, but it's understandable. You come back from a trip and tell me you'd met a woman you wanted to sleep with?

Quentin   That's not the way I said it.

Louise   It's exactly the way. And we were married a year.

Quentin   It is not the way I said it, Louise. It was an idiotic thing to tell you but I still say I meant it as a compliment; that I did not touch her because I realized what you meant to me. And for damn near a year you looked at me as though I were some kind of a monster who could never be trusted again.

Louise   Well that's in *your* mind. I've completely forgotten it.

Quentin   Is it only in my mind if you can still distort it this way?

Louise   Quentin, I am not your mother or some third party to whom you can come running with reports of your conquests!

Quentin   You see? This is what I mean! What conquests? How can I talk if you are going to blow everything up into a – a –

Louise   Quentin, I didn't bring her up, you did.

Quentin   Because I know you have never forgiven it, and I can't talk if I have to watch every word I say.

Louise (*astonished*)   You mean you have to watch every word you say?

Quentin   Well, not every word, but – but –

Louise (*looking at him with new eyes*)   Well, I had no idea!

Quentin (*pleading*)   Now, look, Louise . . . I didn't mean it exactly that way!

Louise (*horrified.*) I had no idea you were . . . dishonest with me.

Quentin (*drowning in guilt*)   Well what did I say? What are you looking at me like that for?

With her hands thrust into her hair she rushes away, a stifled cry in her throat. He calls after her.

Louise!

Immediately to the **Listener***:*

And why do I believe she's right? . . . That's the point! . . . Yes, now, now! It's innocence, isn't it? The innocent are always better, aren't they? Then why can't I be innocent?

Elsie *appears, about to drop her robe.*

Quentin   Why couldn't I simply say, 'Louise, your best friend is treacherous; your newfound dignity suits her purpose'? . . . No, no, it isn't only that Elsie tempted me, it's worse. If I see a sin why is it in some part mine?

Elsie *vanishes as the tower appears.*

Quentin   Even this slaughterhouse! Could I kill Jews? Throw ice water on prisoners of war and let them freeze to death? Why does something in this place touch my shoulder like an accomplice? . . . Huh? Please, yes, if you think you know.

Mother *appears. He turns to her.*

Quentin   In what sense treacherous?

Mother   What poetry he brought me! He understood me, Strauss. And two weeks after the wedding, Papa hands me the menu. To *read*!

Quentin   Huh! Yes! And to a little boy . . . who knows how to read; a powerful reader, that little boy!

Mother   I want your handwriting beautiful, darling; I want you to be . . .

Quentin   . . . an accomplice!

Mother (*turning on* **Father**, *who sits dejectedly*)   My *bonds*? And you don't even tell me anything? Are you a moron?

Quentin (*he watches her go dark, and speaks to the* **Listener**. *The tower remains alive*)   Yes, yes, I understand, but . . . Why is the world so treacherous? Shall we lay it all to mothers? You understand? The sickness is much larger than my skull; aren't there mothers who keep dissatisfaction hidden to the grave, and do not split the faith of sons until they go in guilt for what they did not do? And I'll go further – here's the final bafflement for me – is it altogether good to be not guilty for what another does?

Mickey *appears coming to* **Quentin**, *who turns to him*.

Mickey   The brief is fine, kid; I swear it almost began to move me. (*To* **Louise**, *grinning*.) You proud of him?

Louise (*she starts off*)   Yes! Lou and Elsie are here.

Mickey   Oh! I didn't know. You look wonderful, Louise, look all excited!

Louise   Thanks! It's nice to hear.

She shyly, soundlessly laughs, glancing at **Quentin**, *and goes*.

Mickey (*pause; his smile transforms instantly to a shy grin*)   You got trouble?

Quentin (*embarrassed*)   I don't think so. She's going into psychoanalysis.

The tower dies out.

Mickey   You got trouble, then. (*Laughs*.) But she'll be more interesting. Although for a while she'll probably be talking about her rights.

Quentin   Really? That's just what she was talking about!

Mickey (*shakes his head, laughs joyfully*)   I love women! I think maybe you got married too young; I did too. Although, *you* don't fool around, do you?

Quentin   I don't, no.

Mickey   Then what the hell are you so guilty about?

Quentin   I am?

Mickey   She loves you, Quent.

Quentin   I guess so, ya.

Mickey   Maybe you ought to – See, when it first happened to me, I set aside five minutes a day just imagining my wife as a stranger. As though I hadn't made her yet. You got to generate some respect for her mystery. Start with five minutes; I can go as long as an hour, now.

Quentin   Makes it seem like a game though, doesn't it?

Mickey   Well it is, isn't it, in a way? As soon as there's two people you can't be absolutely sincere, can you? I mean she's not your rib.

Quentin   I guess that's right, yes.

Pause.

Mickey   Where's Lou?

Quentin (*pointing*)   They're down swimming. You want to swim?

Mickey   No.

He walks to a point, looks down as over a cliff.

That dear man; look at him, he never learned how to swim, always paddled like a dog. I used to love that man. I still do.

He sits on his heels, draws in the earth.

I'm sorry you didn't get into town two weeks ago when I called you.

Quentin   Why, is there some . . . ?

Mickey   Well, I called you, Quent, I called you three times wanting to talk to you.

He gets up, stands, hands in pockets, glancing at the ground.

I've been subpoenaed.

Quentin (*shocked*)   Oh, God! The Committee?

Mickey   Yes. I wish you'd have come into town . . . But it doesn't matter now.

Quentin   I had a feeling it was something like that. I guess I . . . didn't want to know any more. I'm sorry, Mick.

To the **Listener**.

Quentin   Yes, not to see, not to see!

A long pause. They find it hard to look directly at each other.

Mickey *picks up a stick, gouges at it with his thumbnail.*

Mickey   I've been going through hell, Quent. It's a strange thing – to have to examine what you stand for; not theoretically, but on a life-and-death basis. A lot of things don't stand up.

Quentin   I guess the main thing is not to be afraid.

Mickey   Yes. (*Pause.*) I don't think I am, any more. I was, two weeks ago; I shook when the marshal came into the office and handed me that pink piece of paper. I really shook. It was dreadful. My knees shook.

A pause. Both sit staring ahead. Finally, **Mickey** *turns and looks at* **Quentin***, who now faces him.* **Mickey** *tries to smile.*

Mickey   You may not be my friend any more.

Quentin (*tries to laugh it away, a terror rising in him*)   Why?

Mickey   I'm going to tell the truth.

Pause.

Quentin   How do you mean?

Mickey   I'm . . . going to name names.

Quentin (*incredulously*)   Why?

Mickey   Because . . . I want to. I don't want this concealment any more. Fifteen years, wherever I go, whatever I talk about, the feeling is always there that I'm deceiving people. Like living in an occupied country, half in the dark.

Quentin   But you only belonged for a few months, didn't you?

Mickey   Yes, but it was a commitment, Quent. I'm sorry we never got to talk about it; I've never really gone along with this Fifth Amendment silence, I think it's insincere; a man ought to take the rap for what he's been.

Quentin   But why couldn't you just tell about yourself?

Mickey   I have. They're playing for keeps, kid; they want the names, and they mean to destroy anyone who –

Quentin   I think it's a mistake, Mick. All this is going to pass, and I think you'll regret it. And anyway, how can they destroy you?

Mickey (*slight pause*)   Quent, I'll be voted out of the firm if I don't testify.

Quentin   Oh, no! Max has always talked against this kind of thing!

Mickey   I've had it out with Max.

Quentin   I can't believe it! What about DeVries?

Mickey   DeVries was there, and Burton, and most of the others. I wish you'd have seen their faces when I told them. Men I've worked with for thirteen years. Played tennis; intimate friends, you know? And as soon as I said I had been – stones.

The tower lights.

Quentin (*to the* **Listener**)   Everything is one thing! You see? I don't know what we are to one another! Or rather, rather what we ought to be!

Mickey   Quent, I could feel their backs turning on me. It was horrible! As though – they would let me die.

Maggie *appears in her bed, and her breathing is heard.*

Maggie   Quentin?

Quentin *barely glances at her and turns away, pacing up and down before the* **Listener***. As* **Mickey** *resumes,* **Maggie** *and her deep-drawn breathing fade away.*

Mickey   I only know one thing, Quent, I want to live an open life, a straightforward, open life!

Lou *enters in bathing trunks, instantly overjoyed at seeing* **Mickey***.*

Lou   Mick! I *thought* I heard your voice! (*Grabs his hand.*) How are you?

Holga *appears beneath the tower with flowers, and in a moment disappears.*

Quentin   How do you dare make promises again? I have lived through all the promises, you see?

Mickey   Pretty good, Lou. I intended to call you tomorrow.

Lou   Really? I was going to call *you*; about a little problem I – (*Uncertain.*) May I?

Mickey   Of course, Lou! You can always call me. I've got guests at home. (*Grasps* **Lou***'s arm.*) Give my best to Elsie.

Lou (*relieved*)   I'll ring you tomorrow! And thank you, Mickey!

The gratitude seems to stab **Mickey***, who is already a few yards away, and he turns back, resolves to turn back.*

Mickey   What . . . was the problem, Lou?

Lou (*relieved, hurrying to him like a puppy*)   Just the question of publishing my book now. Elsie's afraid it will wake up all the sleeping dogs again . . .

Mickey (*pause*)   But don't you have to take that chance? I think a man's got to take the rap, Lou, for what he's done, for what he is. I think what you hide poisons you. After all, it's your work.

Lou   I feel exactly that way! (*Grabs his arm.*) Golly, Mick! Why don't we get together as we used to? I miss all that wonderful talk! Of course I know how busy you are now, but –

Mickey   Lou.

Pause.

Lou   Yes, Mick. I'll meet you anywhere you say!

Mickey   Elsie coming up?

Lou   You want to see her? I could call down to the beach.

He starts off. **Mickey** *stops him.*

Mickey   Lou.

Lou (*sensing something odd*)   Yes, Mick.

Quentin (*facing the sky*)   Dear God.

Mickey   I've been subpoenaed.

Lou   No!

Mickey *nods, looks at the ground.* **Lou** *grips his arm.*

Lou   Oh, I'm terribly sorry, Mick. I was afraid of that when they called me. But can I say something – it might ease your mind: once you're in front of them it all gets remarkably simple!

Quentin   Oh, dear God!

Lou   Really, it's not as terrible as it seems to you now; everything kind of falls away excepting one's . . . one's self. One's truth.

Mickey (*slight pause*)   I've already been in front of them, Lou. Two weeks ago.

Lou   Oh! Then what do they want with you again?

Mickey (*pause. A fixed smile on his face*)   I asked to be heard again.

Lou (*puzzled, open-eyed*)   Why?

Mickey (*he carefully forms his thought*)   Because I want to tell the truth.

Lou (*with the first rising of incredulous fear*)   In . . . what sense? What do you mean?

Mickey   Lou, when I left the hearing room I didn't feel I had spoken. Something else had spoken, something automatic and inhuman. I asked myself, what am I protecting by refusing to answer? Lou, you must let me finish! You must. The Party? But I despise the Party, and have for many years. Just like you. Yet there is something, something that closes my throat when I think of telling names. What am I defending? It's a dream, now, a dream of solidarity, but hasn't that died a long time ago? The fact is, I have no solidarity with the people I could name, excepting for you. And not because we were Communists together, but because we were young together. Because we – when we talked it was like monks probably talk, like some brotherhood opposed to all the world's injustice. It's you made my throat close, just the love whenever we saw one another. But what created that love, Lou? Wasn't it a respect for truth, a hatred of hypocrisy? Therefore, in the name of that love, I ought to be true to myself now. It would be easier, in a sense, to do what you did and stick with it; I would keep your friendship, but lose myself. Because the truth, Lou, my truth, is that I think the Party *is* a conspiracy . . . Let me finish. I think we *were* swindled; they took our lust for the right and used it for Russian purposes. And I don't think we can go on turning our backs on the truth simply because reactionaries are saying it. What I propose – is that we try to separate our love for one another from this political morass. It was not the Party we loved, it was each other's truth. And I've said nothing just now that we haven't told each other for the past five years.

Lou   Then . . . what's your proposal?

Mickey   That we go back together. Come with me. And answer the questions. I was going to tell you this tomorrow.

Lou   Name . . . the names?

Mickey   Yes. I've talked to all the others in the unit. They've agreed, excepting for Ward and Harry. They cursed me out, but I expected that.

Lou (*dazed*)   Let me understand – you are asking my permission to name me? (*Pause.*) You may not mention my name. (*He begins physically shaking.*) And if you do it, Mickey, you are selling me for your own prosperity. If you use my name I will be dismissed. You will ruin me. You will destroy my career.

Mickey   Lou, I think I have a right to know exactly why you –

Lou   Because if everyone broke faith there would be no civilization! That is why that Committee is the face of the Philistine! And it astounds me that you can speak of truth and justice in relation to that gang of cheap publicity hounds! Not one syllable will they get from me! Not one word from my lips! No – your eleven-room apartment, your automobile, your money are not worth this.

He strides toward the edge of the area.

Mickey (*stiffened*)   That's a lie! You can't reduce it all to money, Lou! *That is false!*

Lou (*turning on him*)   There is only one truth here. You are terrified! They have bought your soul!

He starts out again.

Mickey (*angrily, but contained*)   And yours? Lou! Is it all yours, your soul?

Lou (*beginning to show tears*)   How dare you speak of my – ?

Mickey (*quaking with anger*)   You've got to take it if you're going to dish it out, don't you? Have you really earned this high moral tone – this . . .

Elsie *appears in the farthest distance, slowly coming toward them as though from a beach, her robe open, her head raised up toward the breeze, toward longing, toward the sky.*

Mickey   . . . perfect integrity? I happen to remember when you came back from your trip to Russia; and I remember who made you throw your first version into my fireplace!

Lou (*almost screaming – after a glance toward* **Elsie**)   The idea!

Mickey   I saw you burn a true book and write another that told lies! Because she demanded it, because she terrified you, because she has taken your soul!

Lou (*shaking his fist in the air*)   I condemn you!

Mickey   But from your conscience or from hers? Who is speaking to me, Lou?

Lou   You are a monster!

He bursts into tears, walks off toward **Elsie**; *he meets her in the near distance, says a few words, and her face shows horror. At the front of stage* **Mickey** *turns and looks across the full width toward* **Quentin** *at the farthest edge of light, and, reading* **Quentin***'s feelings:*

Mickey   I guess you'll want to get somebody else to go over your brief with you.

Quentin, *indecisive, but not contradicting him, now turns to him.*

Mickey   Good-bye, Quentin.

Quentin (*in a dead tone*)   Good-bye, Mickey.

Mickey *goes out as* **Elsie** *and* **Lou** *rush down, she in a near-hysteria. As they arrive,* **Louise** *appears, stands watching.*

Elsie   Did you hear? (*Including* **Louise** *in her glance.*) Did you hear? He's a *moral idiot*!

Quentin *turns to her; something perhaps in his gaze or in the recesses of her mind makes her close her robe, which she holds tightly shut. And to* **Quentin** . . .

Elsie   Isn't that *incredible*?

Quentin (*quietly*)   Yes.

Elsie   After such friendship! Such love between them! And for so many years!

The camp tower comes alive, and **Quentin** *moves out of this group, slowly toward it, looking up.*

Lou (*stunned*)   And only this spring, brought me an expensive briefcase for my birthday!

Elsie   And named his son Louis after you! Who can understand this?

Above, **Holga** *appears as before, carrying flowers. She is a distance away from* **Quentin***, who turns to her.*

Quentin   You love me, don't you?

Holga   Yes.

An instant's hesitation and he turns quickly to the **Listener***, and cries out.*

Quentin   Is it that I'm looking for some simple-minded constancy that never is and never was?

He turns to **Elsie***, who is lifting* **Lou** *to his feet and kisses him.*

Quentin   How tenderly she lifts him up – now that he is ruined.

Elsie *walks off with* **Lou***, her arm around him, and kissing his cheek.* **Quentin** *watches them go.*

Quentin   Still, that could be a true kiss. Or is there no treason but only man, unblameable as trees or cats or clouds? . . . Yes, I do, I see it; but if that is what we are, what will keep us safe?

Louise *appears.*

Quentin   Or is the question foolish?

Louise   I had a dream. I want to tell you about it.

Quentin (*in pain*)   Are we ever safe?

Louise   I was standing beside a high mountain. With my legs cut off.

He picks up a brief, looks into it.

Must you work tonight?

Quentin   It's Lou's case. I have a pile of stuff. (*Slight pause.*) Well, I can do it later. What is it?

Louise   Never mind.

Quentin (*he sits at once, as though remembering some resolution to act well*)   I'm sorry, Louise. What'd you want to say?

Louise   I'm trying to understand why you got so angry with me at the party the other night . . .

Quentin   I wasn't *angry*; I simply felt that every time I began to talk you cut in to explain what I was about to say.

Louise   Well, I'd had a drink; I was a little high. I felt happy, I guess, that you weren't running for cover when everybody else was.

Quentin   Yes, but Max was there, and DeVries, and they don't feel they're running for cover. I only want to win Lou's case, not some moral victory over the firm. I felt you were putting me out on a limb.

Louise   Quentin, I saw you getting angry when I was talking about that new anti-virus vaccine.

He tries to remember, believing she is right.

What is it? Don't you want me to speak at all?

Quentin   That's ridiculous, Louise, why do you –

Louise   Because the moment I begin to assert myself it seems to threaten you. I don't think you *want* me to be happy.

Quentin (*there is a basic concession made by his tone of admitted bewilderment*)   I tell you the truth, Louise – I don't think I feel very sure of myself any more. I feel sometimes that I don't see reality at all. I'm glad I took on Lou, but it only hit me lately that no respectable lawyer would touch him. It's like some unseen web of connection between people is simply not there. And I always relied on it, somehow; I never quite believed that people could be so easily disposed of. And it's larger than the political question. I think it's got me a little scared.

Louise (*with a wish for his sympathy, not accusing*)   Well then, you must know how I felt when I found that letter in your suit.

Quentin (*he turns to her, aware*)   I didn't do that to dispose of you, Louise.

She does not reply.

I thought we'd settled about that girl.

She still does not reply.

You mean you think I'm still . . .

Louise   I don't know what you're doing.

Quentin (*astounded*)   What do you mean, you don't know?

Louise (*directly at him*)   I said I don't know! I thought you told the truth about the other girl years ago, but after what happened again this spring – I don't know anything.

Quentin (*pause*)   Tell me something; until this party the other night – in fact this whole year – I thought you seemed much happier. You were, weren't you?

Louise   Quentin, aren't you aware I've simply been staying out of your way this year?

Quentin (*amazed, frightened for his sense of reality*)   Staying out of my way!

Louise   Well, can you remember one thing I've said about myself this year?

Quentin (*angrily, still amazed*)   I swear to God, Louise, I thought we were building something till the other night!

Louise   But why?

Quentin   Well, I can't give you a bill of particulars, but it seems pretty obvious I've been trying like hell to show what I think of you. You've seen that, haven't you?

Louise   Quentin, you are full of resentment; you think I'm blind?

Quentin   What I resent is being forever on trial, Louise. Are you an innocent bystander here? I keep waiting for some contribution you might have made to what I did, and I resent not hearing it.

Louise   I said I did contribute; I demanded nothing for much too long.

Quentin   You mean the summer before last you didn't come to me and say that if I didn't change you would divorce me?

Louise   I never said I was *planning* a –

Quentin   You said if it came down to it you would divorce me – that's not a contribution?

Louise   Well, it certainly ought not send a man out to play doctor with the first girl he could lay his hands on!

Quentin   How much shame do you want me to feel? I hate what I did. But I think I've explained it – I felt like nothing; I shouldn't have, but I did, and I took the only means I knew to –

Louise   This is exactly what I mean, Quentin – you are still defending it. Right now.

He is stopped by this truth.

And I know it, Quentin.

Quentin   And you're . . . not at all to blame, heh?

Louise   But how?

Quentin   Well, for example . . . you never turn your back on me in bed?

Louise   I never turned my –

Quentin   You have turned your back on me in bed, Louise. I am not insane!

Louise   Well what do you expect? Silent, cold, you lay your hand on me?

Quentin (*fallen*)   Well, I . . . I'm not very demonstrative, I guess.

Slight pause. He throws himself on her compassion.

Louise . . . I worry about you all day. And all night.

Louise (*it is something, but not enough*)   Well, you've got a child; I'm sure that worries you.

Quentin (*deeply hurt*)   Is that all?

Louise (*with intense reasonableness*)   Look, Quentin, it all comes down to a very simple thing; you want a woman to provide an . . . atmosphere, in which there are never any issues, and you'll fly around in a constant bath of praise . . .

Quentin   Well I wouldn't mind a little praise, what's wrong with praise?

Louise   Quentin, I am not a praise machine! I am not a blur and I am not your mother! I am a separate person!

Quentin (*he stares at her, and what lies beyond her*)   I see that now.

Louise   It's no crime! Not if you're adult and grown-up.

Quentin (*quietly*)   I guess not. But it bewilders me. In fact, I got the same idea when I realized that Lou had gone from one of his former students to another and none would take him . . .

Louise   What's Lou got to do with it? I think it's admirable that you . . .

Quentin   Yes, but I am doing what you call an admirable thing because I can't bear to be a separate person! I think so. I really don't want to be known as a Red lawyer; and I really don't want the newspapers to eat me alive; and if it came down to it, Lou could defend himself. But when that decent, broken man, who never wanted anything but the good of the

world, sits across my desk . . . I don't know how to say that my
interests are no longer the same as his, and that if he doesn't
change I consign him to hell because we are separate persons.

Louise   You are completely confused! Lou's case has nothing –

Quentin (*grasping for his thought*)   I am telling you my
confusion! I think Mickey also became a separate person.

Louise   You're incredible!

Quentin   I think of my mother, I think she also became –

Louise   Are you identifying *me* with –

Quentin   Louise, I am asking you to explain this to me
because this is when I go blind! When you've finally become
a separate person, what the hell is there?

Louise (*with a certain unsteady pride*)   Maturity.

Quentin   I don't know what that means.

Louise   It means that you know another person exists,
Quentin. I'm not in analysis for nothing!

Quentin (*questing*)   It's probably the symptom of a typical
case of some kind, but I swear, Louise – if you would just
once, of your own will, as right as you are – if you would come
to me and say that something, something important was your
fault and that you were sorry . . . it would help.

In her pride she is silent, in her refusal to be brought down again.

Louise?

Louise   Good God! What an idiot!

*She begins to weep helplessly for her life, and vanishes. Light rises on a
park bench with the sound of traffic. A young Negro hurries past, neat,
wearing sunglasses, on the lookout, halts to flick dust off his shined shoes,
goes on. An old woman in shapeless dress carries a shopping bag and a
parrot in a cage across, limping.* **Quentin** *strolls on and sits on the
bench, briefcase on his lap.*

Quentin   How few the days are that hold the mind in place; like a tapestry hanging on four or five hooks. Especially the day you stop becoming; the day you merely are. I suppose it's when the principles dissolve, and instead of the general gray of what ought to be you begin to see what is. Even the bench by the park seems alive, having held so many actual men. The word 'Now' is like a bomb through the window, and it ticks.

The old woman recrosses with the parrot.

Now a woman takes a parrot for a walk. Everything suddenly has consequences; she probably worries what will happen to it when she's gone.

A plain girl in tweeds passes, reading a paperback.

And how brave a homely woman has to be! How disciplined of her, not to set fire to the museum of art.

The Negro passes, flicking dust off his shoe, comes to **Quentin** *demanding a light for his cigarette.* **Quentin** *lights it.*

And how does he keep so neat, and the bathroom on another floor? He must be furious when he shaves.

The Negro sees his girl upstage, walks off with her.

And whatever made me think that at the end of the day, I absolutely had to go home? You understand? That day when, suddenly, nothing whatsoever is ordained. Only . . . 'Now', ticking away.

Maggie *appears, looking about for someone.*

Quentin   Now there's a truth; symmetrical, lovely skin, undeniable.

Maggie   S'uze me, did you see a man with a big dog?

Quentin   No. But I saw a woman with a little bird.

Maggie   No, that's not him. Is this the bus stop?

Quentin   Ya, the sign says . . .

Maggie (*sits beside him*)   I was standing over there and a man came with this big dog and just put the leash in my hand and walked away. So I started to go after him but the dog wouldn't move. And then this other man came and took the leash and went away. But I don't think it's really his dog. I think it's the first man's dog.

Quentin   But he obviously doesn't want it.

Maggie   But maybe he wanted for me to have it. I think the other man just saw it happening and figured he could get a free dog.

Quentin   Well, you want the dog?

Maggie   How could I keep a dog? I don't even think they allow dogs where I live. They might, but I never saw any dog. Although I'm not there much. What bus is this?

Quentin   Fifth Avenue. This is the downtown side. Where did you want to go?

Maggie (*thinks*)   Well, I could go there.

Quentin   Where?

Maggie   Downtown.

Quentin   Lot of funny things go on, don't they?

Maggie   Well, he probably figured I would like a dog. Whereas I would if I had a way to keep it, but I don't even have a refrigerator.

Quentin   Yes. (*Pause.*) I guess he thought you had a refrigerator; that must be it.

She shrugs. Pause. He looks at her as she watches for the bus. He has no more to say. **Louise** *lights up.*

Louise   You don't talk to any woman – not like a *woman*! You think reading your brief is *talking* to me?

She goes dark. In tension **Quentin** *leans forward, arms resting on his knees. He looks at* **Maggie** *again. Anonymous men appear, lounge about, eying her.*

Quentin (*with an effort*)   What do you do?

Maggie (*as though he should know*)   On the switchboard.

Quentin   Oh, telephone operator?

Maggie (*laughs*)   Don't you remember me?

Quentin (*surprised*)   Me?

Maggie   I always sort of nod to you every morning through the window.

Quentin (*an instant*)   Oh. In the reception room!

Maggie   Sure!

Quentin   What's your name?

Maggie   Maggie.

Quentin   Of course! You get my numbers sometimes.

Maggie   Did you think I just came up and started talking to you?

Quentin   I had no idea.

Maggie (*laughs*)   Well what must you have thought!

Quentin   I didn't know what to think.

Maggie   I guess it's that you never saw me altogether. I mean just my head through that little window.

Quentin   Yes. Well, it's nice to meet all of you, finally.

Maggie (*laughs*)   You go back to work again tonight?

Quentin   No, I'm just resting for a few minutes.

Maggie (*with a sense of his loneliness*)   Oh.

She looks idly about. He glances down her body.

Quentin   It's a pity you have to sit behind that little window.

She laughs, gratefully. Her eye catches something.

Maggie (*rising*)   Is that my bus down there?

Quentin   I'm not really sure where you want to go.

A man appears, eyes her, glances up toward the bus, back to her, staring.

Maggie   I wanted to find one of those discount stores; I just bought a phonograph but I only have one record. I'll see you!

She is half-backing off toward the man.

Man   There's one on Twenty-Seventh and Sixth Avenue.

Maggie (*turning, surprised*)   Oh, thanks!

Quentin (*standing; moving toward her as though not to lose her to the man*)   There's a record store around the corner, you know.

Maggie   But is it discount?

Quentin   Well they all discount –

Man (*slipping his hand under her arm*)   What, ten per cent? Come on, honey, I'll get you easy fifty off.

Maggie (*moving off on his arm*)   Really? But Perry Sullivan?

Man   Look, I'll give it to you – I'll give you two records! Come on!

Maggie (*she halts, suddenly aware; disengages her arm, backs off*) S'uze me, I . . . I . . . forgot something.

Man (*lathering*)   Look, I'll give you ten records. (*Calls off.*) Hold that door! (*Grabs her.*) Come on!

Quentin (*moving toward him*)   Hey!

Man (*letting her go – to* **Quentin**)   Ah, get lost! (*He rushes off.*) Hold it, hold the door!

Quentin *watches the bus go by, then turns to her. She is absorbed in arranging her hair – but with a strangely doughy expression, removed.*

Quentin   I'm sorry, I thought you knew him.

Maggie   No. I never saw him.

Quentin   Well . . . what were you going with him for?

Maggie   Well he said he knew a store.

Quentin (*mystified, intrigued, looks at her, then nods inconclusively*)
Oh.

Maggie   Where's the one you're talking about?

Quentin   I'll have to think a minute. Let's see . . .

Maggie   Could I sit with you? While you're thinking?

Quentin   Sure.

They return to the bench. He waits till she is seated; she is aware of the politeness, glances at him as he sits. Then she looks at him fully, for some reason amazed.

That happen to you very often?

Maggie   Pretty often.

It is impossible to tell if she likes it or not.

Quentin   It's because you talk to them.

Maggie   But they talk to me, so I have to answer.

Quentin   Not if they're rude.

Maggie   But if they talk to me . . .

Quentin   Just turn your back.

Maggie (*she thinks about that, and indecisively*)   Oh, okay. (*As though remotely aware of another world, his world.*) . . . Thanks, though . . . for stopping it.

Quentin   Well, anybody would.

Maggie   No, they laugh. It's a joke to them. (*She laughs in pain. Slight pause.*) You . . . going to rest here very long?

Quentin   Just a few minutes. I'm on my way home. I never did this before.

Maggie   Oh! You look like you always did.

Quentin   Why?

Maggie   I don't know. You look like you could sit for hours, under these trees . . . just thinking.

Quentin   No. I usually go right home. (*Grinning.*) I've always gone right home.

Maggie (*she absorbs this*)   Oh. (*Coming awake.*) See, I'm still paying for the phonograph, whereas they don't sell records on time, you know.

Quentin   They're afraid they'll wear out, I guess.

Maggie   Oh, that must be it! I always wondered. 'Cause you *can* get phonographs. How'd you know that?

Quentin   I don't. I'm just guessing.

Maggie   It sounds true, though. (*Laughs.*) I can never guess those things! I don't know why they do anything half the time! (*She laughs more deeply. He does.*) I had about ten or twenty records in Washington, but my friend got sick, and I had to leave. Although maybe they're still there.

Quentin   Well, if you still have the apartment . . .

Maggie   I'm not sure I do. I got a letter from them couple months ago, the Real Estate. (*Pause. Thinks.*) I better open it. He lived right over there on Park Avenue.

Quentin   Oh. Is he better?

Maggie   He died. (*Tears come into her eyes.*)

Quentin (*entirely perplexed*)   When was this?

Maggie   Friday. Remember they closed the office for the day?

Quentin   You mean – (*Astounded.*) Judge Cruse?

Maggie   Ya.

Quentin (*with lingering surprise*)   Oh, I didn't know that you . . . He was a great lawyer. And a great judge, too.

Maggie (*rubbing tears*)   He was very nice to me.

Quentin   I was at the funeral; I didn't see you, though.

Maggie (*with difficulty against her tears*)   His wife wouldn't let me come. But I got into the hospital before he died. But as soon as I opened the door of his room the family pushed me out and . . . I could hear him calling, 'Maggie! Maggie!' (*Pause.*) They kept trying to offer me a thousand dollars. But I told them, I don't want anything, I just wanted to say good-bye to him!

She opens her purse, takes out an office envelope, opens it.

I have a little of the dirt. See? That's from his grave. His chauffeur drove me out – Alexander.

Quentin (*looks at the dirt, at her face*)   Did he leave you very much?

Maggie   No, he didn't leave me anything.

She puts the envelope back, closes the purse, stares.

Quentin   Did you love him very much?

Maggie   No. But he was very nice. In fact, a couple of times I really left him.

Quentin   Why didn't you altogether?

Maggie   He didn't want me to.

Quentin   Oh. (*Pause.*) So what are you going to do now?

Maggie   I'd love to get that record if I knew where they had a discount.

Quentin   No, I mean in general.

Maggie   Why, they going to fire me now?

Quentin   Oh, I wouldn't know about that.

Maggie   Although I'm not worried, whereas I can always go back to hair.

Quentin   To where?

Maggie   I used to demonstrate hair preparations. (*Laughs, squirts her hair with an imaginary bottle.*) You know, in department stores? I was traveling even, they sent me to Boston and New Orleans and all over. (*Tilting her head under his chin.*) It's because I have very thick hair, you see? I have my mother's hair. And it's not broken. You notice I have no broken hair? Most women's hair is broken. Here, feel it, feel how – (*She has lifted his hand to her head, and suddenly lets go of it.*) Oh, s'uze me!

Quentin   That's all right.

Maggie   I just thought you might want to feel it.

Quentin   Sure.

Maggie   Go ahead. I mean if you want to.

She leans her head to him again. He touches the top of her head.

Quentin   It is, ya! Very soft.

Maggie (*proudly*)   I once went from page boy to bouffant in less than ten minutes!

Quentin   What made you quit?

Maggie (*the dough comes into her eyes again*)   They start sending me to conventions and all. You're supposed to entertain, you see.

Quentin   Oh, yes.

Maggie   There were parts of it I didn't like any more.

A long moment. A student goes by, reading. He looks up from his book, shyly glances at her, goes on reading. She laughs.

Aren't they sweet when they look up from their books!

She turns to him with a laugh. He looks at her warmly, smiling.

S'uze me I put your hand on my head.

Quentin   Oh, that's all right . . . I'm not *that* bad. (*He laughs softly, embarrassed.*)

Maggie   You're not bad.

Quentin   I don't mean bad, I mean . . . shy.

Maggie   It's not bad to be shy. (*She gives him a long look, absorbed.*) I mean . . . if that's the way you are.

Quentin   I guess I am, then.

Pause. They look at each other.

You're very beautiful, Maggie.

She smiles, straightens as though his words had entered her.

And I wish you knew how to take care of yourself.

Maggie   Oh . . . (*Holding out a ripped seam in her dress.*) I got this torn on the bus this morning. I'm going to sew it home.

Quentin   I don't mean that.

She meets his eyes again – she looks chastised.

Not that I'm criticizing you. I'm not at all. Not in the slightest. You understand?

She nods, absorbed in his face. He stands.

I've got to go now.

She stands, staring at him, giving herself. He sees this. His hand moves, but it becomes a handshake.

You could look up record stores in the phone book.

Maggie   I think I'll take a walk in the park.

Quentin   You shouldn't. It's getting dark.

Maggie   But it's beautiful at night. I slept there one night when it was hot in my room.

Quentin   God, you don't want to do that! I know this park. Most of the animals are not in the zoo.

Maggie   Okay. I'll get a record, then. (*She backs a step.*) S'uze me about my hair if I embarrassed you.

Quentin (*laughs*)   You didn't.

Maggie (*backing to leave, she touches the top of her head*)   It's just that it's not broken.

He nods. She halts some yards away, holds out her torn seam.

I'm going to sew this home.

He nods. She indicates the park, upstage.

I didn't *mean* to sleep there. I just fell asleep.

Two young guys appear, pass **Quentin**, *slow as they pass her, and halt in the far periphery of the light, waiting for her.*

Quentin   I understand.

Maggie   Well . . . see you! (*Laughs.*) If they don't fire me!

Quentin   Bye.

She passes the two men, who walk step for step behind her, whispering in her ear together. She doesn't turn or answer but shows no surprise.

Quentin (*in anguish he hurries after her*)   Maggie! (*He catches her arm and brings her clear of the men, takes a bill from his pocket.*) Here, why don't you take a cab? It's on me. Go ahead, there's one right there. (*Points and whistles.*) Go on, grab it!

Maggie (*backing in the opposite direction from the waiting men*) Where . . . where will I tell him to go but?

Quentin   Just cruise in the forties – you've got enough there.

Maggie   Okay, bye! (*Backing out.*) You . . . you just going to rest more?

Quentin   I don't know.

Maggie (*wondrously*)   Golly, that's nice!

She hurries off. He stands staring after her. Likewise, the men watch the cab going by, then walk off.

Lights rise on **Louise** *reading in a chair.* **Quentin**, *clasping his briefcase behind his back, walks slowly into the area, stands a few yards from her, staring at her. She remains unaware of him, reading and smoking.*

Quentin   Yes. She has legs, breasts, mouth, eyes. How wonderful – a woman of my own! What a miracle! In my own house!

He walks to her, bends and kisses her. She looks up at him surprised, perplexed.

Hi.

She keeps looking up at him, aware of some sea-like opening in the world.

What's the matter?

She still doesn't speak.

Well, what's the matter?

Louise   Nothing.

She returns to her book. Mystified, disappointed, he stands watching, then opens his briefcase and begins taking out papers.

Close the door if you're going to type.

Quentin   I always do.

Louise   Not always.

Quentin   Almost always.

He almost laughs, he feels loose, but she won't be amused, and returns again to her book. He starts for the bedroom, halts.

How about eating out tomorrow night? Before the parents' meeting?

Louise   What parents' meeting?

Quentin   The school.

Louise   That was tonight.

Quentin (*shocked*)   Really?

Louise   Of course. I just got back.

Quentin   Why didn't you remind me when I called today?

Louise   You knew it as well as I.

Quentin   But you know I often forget those things. I told you I wanted to talk to her teacher.

Louise (*a little more sharply*)   People do what they want to do, Quentin.

Quentin   But Louise, I was talking to you at three o'clock this afternoon . . .

Louise (*an unwilling shout*)   Because you said you had to work tonight!

She glares at him meaningfully; returns to her book. He stands, alarmed.

Quentin   I didn't work.

Louise (*keeping to her book*)   *I* know you didn't work.

Quentin (*surprised*)   How did you know?

Louise   Well for one thing, Max called here at seven-thirty.

Quentin   Max? What for?

Louise   Apparently the whole executive committee was in his office waiting to meet with you tonight.

His hand goes to his head; open alarm shows on his face.

He called three times, as a matter of fact.

Quentin   I forgot all about it! (*He hurries to the phone, stops.*) How is that possible? It completely –

Louise   Well they wouldn't be there any more now. (*Pointedly.*) It's ten-thirty.

Quentin   My God, I – How could I do that? What's his home number?

Louise   The book is in the bedroom.

Quentin   We were supposed to discuss my handling Lou's case. DeVries stayed in town tonight just to . . . settle everything. And I go and walk out as though . . . nothing . . . (*Breaks off. Picks up phone.*) What's Max's number, Murray Hill 3 . . . what is it?

Louise   The book is next to the bed.

Quentin   You remember it, Murray Hill 3, something.

Louise   It's in the book.

Pause. He looks at her. Puzzled.

Quentin   What are you doing?

Louise   I'm saying the book is in the bedroom.

Quentin (*slams the phone down, and, as much in fright as in anger*) But you remember his number!

Louise   I'm not the keeper of your phone numbers. You can remember them just as well as I.

Quentin   Oh, I see. (*Nods ironically, starts out.*)

Louise   Please don't use that phone, you'll wake her up.

Quentin (*turns*)   I had no intention of calling in there.

Louise   I thought you might want to be private.

Quentin   There's nothing private about this. This concerns you as much as me. The food in your mouth and the clothes on your back.

Louise   Really! When did you start thinking of us?

Quentin   The meeting was called to decide whether I should separate from the firm until Lou's case is over – or permanently, for all I know.

He goes toward the phone. She stands staring in growing fright.

Murray Hill 3 . . .

He picks it up, dials one digit.

Louise (*much against her will*)   That's the old number.

Quentin   Murray Hill 3-4598.

Louise   It's been changed. (*A moment; and finally:*) Cortland 7-7098.

Quentin (*she is not facing him; he senses what he thinks is victory*)
Thanks.

Starts again to dial, puts down the phone. She sits; there is an admission of the faintest sort of failing in her.

I don't know what to say to him.

She is silent.

We arranged for everybody to come back after dinner. It'll sound idiotic that I forgot about it.

Louise   You were probably frightened.

Quentin   But I made notes all afternoon about what I would say tonight! It's incredible!

Louise (*with an over-meaning*)   You probably don't realize how frightened you are.

Quentin   I guess I don't. He said a dreadful thing today – Max. He was trying to argue me into dropping Lou and I said, 'The law is the law; we can't adopt some new behavior just because there's hysteria in the country.' I thought it was a perfectly ordinary thing to say but he – he's never looked at me that way – like we were suddenly standing on two distant mountains; and he said, 'I don't know of any hysteria. Not in this office.'

Louise (*without rancor*)   But why does all that surprise you?

Quentin (*slight pause*)   I don't understand exactly what you're getting at.

Louise   Simply that there are some issues you have to face. You tend to make relatives out of people. Max is not your father, or your brother, or anything but a very important lawyer with his own interests. He's not going to endanger his whole firm to defend a Communist. I don't know how you got that illusion.

Quentin   You mean –

Louise   I mean you can't have everything; if you feel this strongly about Lou you probably will have to resign.

Quentin (*pause*)   You think I should?

Louise   That depends on how deeply you feel about Lou.

Quentin   I'm trying to determine that; I don't know for sure. What do you think?

Louise (*in anguish*)   It's not my decision, Quentin.

Quentin (*puzzled and surprised*)   But aren't you involved?

Louise   Of course I'm involved.

Quentin (*genuinely foxed*)   Is it that you're not sure of how you feel?

Louise   I know how I feel but it is not my decision.

Quentin   I'm only curious how you –

Louise   You? Curious about me?

Quentin   Oh. We're not talking about what we're talking about, are we?

Louise (*nodding in emphasis*)   You have to decide what you feel about a certain human being. For once in your life. And then maybe you'll decide what you feel about other human beings. Clearly and decisively.

Quentin   In other words . . . where was I tonight.

Louise   I don't care where you were tonight.

Quentin (*pause*)   I sat by the park for a while. And this is what I thought. I don't sleep with other women, but I think I behave as though I do.

She is listening. He sees it, is enlivened by hope.

Maybe I invite your suspicion on myself in order to . . . to come down off some bench, to stop judging others so perfectly. Because I do judge, and harshly, too – when the fact is I'm bewildered. I even wonder if I left that letter for you to read . . .

about that girl . . . in order to . . . somehow join the condemned;
in some way to start being real. Can you understand that?

Louise   But . . . (*She is digging in her heels against being taken.*)
Why should you be condemned if you're not still doing
anything?

Quentin (*uneasily again*)   But don't you continue to feel
ashamed for something you've done in the past? You can
understand that, can't you?

Louise   I don't do things I'll be ashamed of.

Quentin (*now astonished, and moving toward anger*)   Really and
truly?

Louise (*starts to rise*)   I'm going to bed.

Quentin   I have to say it, Louise; whenever our conversations
verge on you, they end. You say you want to talk, but is it only
about my sins?

Louise   Now you listen here! You've been 'at the office' one
night a week since last winter. It's not my forgiveness you want,
it's the end of this marriage! But you haven't the courage to
say so!

Quentin   All right, then. (*Against his own trepidation, striving for
a clear conscience.*) I think I won't be ashamed either. I met a girl
tonight. Just happened to come by, one of the phone operators
in the office. I probably shouldn't tell you this either, but I will.

She sits, slowly.

Quite stupid, silly kid. Sleeps in the park, her dress is ripped;
she said some ridiculous things, but one thing struck me, she
wasn't defending anything, upholding anything, or accusing –
she was just *there*, like a tree or a cat. And I felt strangely
abstract beside her. And I saw that we are killing one another
with abstractions. I'm defending Lou because I love him, yet
the society transforms that love into a kind of treason, what
they call an issue, and I end up suspect and hated. Why can't
we speak below the 'issues' – with our real uncertainty? I
walked in just now – and I had a tremendous wish to come

out – to you. And you to me. It sounds absurd that this city is full of people rushing to meet one another, Louise. This city is full of lovers . . .

Louise   And what did she say?

Quentin   I guess I shouldn't have told you about it.

Louise   Why not?

Quentin   Louise, I don't know what's permissible to say any more.

Louise (*nods*)   You don't know how much to hide.

Quentin (*he angers*)   All right, let's not hide anything, it would have been easy to make love to her.

Louise *reddens, stiffens.*

Quentin   And I didn't because I thought of you, and in a new way . . . like a stranger I had never gotten to know. And by some miracle you were waiting for me, in my own home. I came into this room, Louise, full of love . . .

Louise   What do you want, my congratulations? You expect me to sit here and enjoy your latest conquest? You take me for a lesbian?

Quentin (*perplexed*)   What's a lesbian got to do with . . .

Louise   Ask your friend with the torn dress. You don't imagine a real woman goes to bed with any man who happens to come along? Or that a real man goes to bed with every woman who'll have him? Especially a slut, which she obviously is?

Quentin   How do you know she's a –

Louise (*laughs*)   Oh, excuse me, I didn't mean to insult her! You're unbelievable! Supposing I came home and told you I'd met a man – a man on the street I wanted to go to bed with . . .

He hangs his head, defeated.

. . . because he made the city seem full of lovers. What would you feel? Overjoyed for my discovery?

Quentin (*pause; struck*)   I understand. I'm sorry. I guess it would anger me too. (*Slight pause.*) But if you came to me with such a thing, I think I would see that you were struggling. And I would ask myself – maybe I'd even be brave enough to ask you – how *I* had failed.

Louise   Well, you've given me notice; I get the message.

She starts out.

Quentin   Louise, don't you ever doubt yourself?

She slows, but does not turn.

Is it enough to prove a case, to even win it – (*Shouts.*) when we are dying?

Louise (*turns in full possession*)   I'm not dying. I'm not the one who wanted to break this up. And that's all it's about. It's all it's been about the last three years. You don't want me!

She goes out.

Quentin   God! Can that be true?

Mickey *enters as he was in his scene, dressed in summer slacks.*

Mickey   There's only one thing I can tell you for sure, kid – don't ever be guilty.

Quentin   Yes! (*Seeking strength, he stretches upward.*) Yes! (*But his conviction wavers; he turns toward the vision.*) But if you had felt more guilt, maybe you wouldn't have . . .

Elsie *rushes into this light as before, her robe open to her tight bathing suit.*

Elsie   He's a moral idiot!

Quentin   Yes! That is right. And yet . . .

He turns and faces her, and she slowly, under his gaze, draws her robe together in a way to conceal her own betrayal, and she and **Mickey** *are gone.* **Quentin** *stands staring out.*

Quentin   What the hell is moral? What does that really mean? And what am I . . . to even ask that question? A man ought to know . . . a decent man knows that like he knows his own face!

Louise *enters with a folded sheet and a pillow which she tosses into the chair.*

Louise   I don't want to sleep with you.

Quentin   Louise, for God's sake!

Louise   You are disgusting!

Quentin   But in the morning Betty will see . . .

Louise   You should have thought of that.

The phone rings. He makes no move to answer.

Did you give her this number?

The phone rings again.

Did you give her this number? (*With which she strides to the phone.*) Hello! . . . Oh, yes. He's here. Hold on, please. (*To him.*) It's Max.

For a moment, he stands touching the sheets, then looks at her, picks up the sheets, and hands them to her.

Quentin   I can't sleep out here; I don't want her to see it.

But she adamantly lets the sheets fall to the floor. He goes to the phone with a look of hatred.

Max? I'm sorry, the whole thing just slipped my mind. I don't know how to explain it, Max, I just went blank, I guess, I – (*Pause.*) The radio? No, why? *What?* When? (*Long pause.*) Thanks . . . for letting me know. Yes, he was. Good night . . . ya, see you in the morning. (*Pause. He stands staring.*)

Louise   What is it?

Quentin   Lou. Was killed by a subway train tonight.

Louise (*gasps*)   How?

Quentin   They don't know. They say 'fell or jumped'.

Louise   He couldn't have! The crowd must have pushed him!

Quentin   There is no crowd at eight o'clock. It was eight o'clock.

Louise   But *why*? Lou *knew* himself! He knew where he *stood*! It's impossible!

Quentin (*staring*)   Maybe it's not enough – to know yourself. Or maybe it's too much. I think he did it.

Louise   But *why*? It's inconceivable!

Quentin   When I saw him last week he said a dreadful thing. I tried not to hear it.

Louise   What?

Quentin   That I turned out to be the only friend he had.

Louise (*genuinely*)   Why is that dreadful?

Quentin (*evasively, almost slyly*)   It just was. (*He starts moving.*) I don't know why.

He arrives at the edge of the stage, tears forming in his eyes.

I didn't dare know why! But I dare now. It was dreadful because I was not his friend either, and he knew it. I'd have stuck it to the end but I hated the danger in it for myself, and he saw through my faithfulness; and he was not telling me what a friend I was, he was praying I would be – 'Please be my friend, Quentin,' is what he was saying to me, 'I am drowning, throw me a rope!' Because I wanted out, to be a good American again, kosher again – and he saw it, and proved it in the joy . . . the joy . . . the joy I felt now that my danger had spilled out on the subway track! So it is not bizarre to me . . .

The tower blazes into life, and he walks with his eyes up. **Holga** *appears with flowers.*

Quentin   This is not some crazy aberration of human nature to me. I can easily see the perfectly normal contractors and their cigars; the carpenters, plumbers, sitting at their ease over lunch pails, I can see them laying the pipes to run the blood out of this mansion; good fathers, devoted sons, grateful that someone else will die, not they. And how can one understand that, if one is innocent; if somewhere in the soul there is no accomplice . . .

The tower fades, **Holga** *too.* **Louise** *brightens in light where she was standing before.*

Quentin   . . . of that joy, that joy, that joy when a burden dies . . .

He moves back into the 'room'.

. . . and leaves you safe?

Maggie's *breathing is heard.*

Maggie   Quentin?

He turns in pain from it, comes to a halt on one side of the sheets and pillow lying on the floor. **Louise** *is on the other side. He looks down at the pile.*

Quentin   I've got to sleep; I'm very tired.

He bends to pick up the sheets. A split second later she starts to. And while he is still reaching down . . .

Louise (*with great difficulty*)   I . . .

He stands with the sheets in hand, the pillow still on the floor; now he is attending her, sensing a confession.

I've always been proud you took Lou's case.

He barely nods, waiting.

It was . . .

She picks up the pillow.

. . . courageous.

She stands there with the pillow, not fully looking at him.

Quentin   I'm glad you feel that way.

But he makes no move. The seconds are ticking by. Neither can let down his demand for apology, for grace. With difficulty.

And that you told me. Thanks.

Louise   You are honest that way. I've often told you.

Quentin   Recently?

Louise (*bridles, hands him the pillow*)   Good night.

He takes the pillow; she starts away, and he feels the unwillingness with which she leaves.

Quentin   Louise, if there's one thing I've been trying to do it's to be honest with you.

Louise   No. You've been trying to arrange things, that's all – to keep the home fires burning and see the world at the same time.

Quentin   So that all I am is deceptive, and cunning.

Louise   Not all, but mostly.

Quentin   And there is no struggle. There is no pain. There is no struggle to find a way back to you?

Louise   That isn't the struggle.

Quentin   Then what are you doing here?

Louise   I . . .

Quentin   What the hell are you compromising yourself for if you're so goddamned honest?

On the line he starts a frustrated clench-fisted move toward her and she backs away, terrified, and strangely alive. Her look takes note of the aborted violence and she is very straight and yet ready to flee.

Louise   I've been waiting for the struggle to begin.

He is dumbstruck – by her sincerity, her adamance. With a straight look at him, she turns and goes out.

Quentin (*alone, and to himself*)   Good God, can there be more? Can there be worse? (*Turning to the* **Listener**.) See, that's what's incredible to me – three years more! What did I expect to save us? Suddenly, God knows why, she'd hold out her hand and I hold out mine, and laugh, laugh it all away, laugh it all back to . . . her dear, honest face looking up to mine . . .

Breaks off, staring.

Back to some hidden, everlasting smile that saves. That's maybe why I came; I think I still believe it. That underneath we're all profoundly friends! I can't believe this world; all this hatred isn't real to me!

Turns back to his 'living-room', and the sheets.

To bed down like a dog in my living room, how can that be necessary? Then go in to her, open your heart, confess the lechery, the mystery of women, say it all . . . the truth must save!

He has moved toward where she exited, now halts.

But I did that. So the truth, after all, may merely be murderous? The truth killed Lou; destroyed Mickey. Then what else is there? A workable lie? Maybe there is only one sin, to destroy your own credibility. Strength comes from a clear conscience or a dead one. Not to see one's own evil – there's power! And rightness too! So kill conscience. Kill it.

Glancing toward her exit.

Know all, admit nothing, shave closely, remember birthdays, open car doors, pursue Louise not with truth but with attention. Be uncertain on your own time, in bed be absolute. And thus, be a man . . . and join the world.

Reflectively he throws the sheet open on the couch, then stops.

And in the morning, a dagger in that dear little daughter's heart!

Flinging it toward **Louise***'s exit.*

Bitch!

Sits.

I'll say I have a cold. Didn't want to give it to Mommy.

With disgust.

Pah! Papapapapa.

Sniffs, tries to talk through his nose.

Got a cold in my dose, baby girl . . .

He groans. Pause. He stares; stalemate. A jet plane is heard. An airport porter appears, unloads two bags from a rolling cart as **Holga**, *dressed for travel, appears opening her purse, tipping him, and now looking about for* **Quentin**. *A distant jet roars in take-off.* **Quentin** *glances at his watch, and, coming down to the chair:*

Quentin   Six o'clock, Idlewild.

Now he glances at **Holga**, *who is still looking about him as in a crowd, and speaks to the* **Listener**.

Quentin   It's that the evidence is bad for promises. But how do you touch the world without a promise? And yet, I mustn't forget the way I wake; I open up my eyes each morning like a boy, even now, even now! That's as true as anything I know, but where's the evidence? Or is it simply that my heart still beats? . . . Certainly, go ahead.

He smiles and sits, following the departing **Listener** *with his eyes; a light moves upstage, going away. He talks upstage.*

Quentin   You don't mind my staying? Good. I'd like to settle this. Although actually, I – (*Laughs.*) only came by to say hello.

He turns front. The **Listener**'s *light is gone. Alone now, he stares ahead, a different kind of relaxation on him. From the darkness high on the upper level, the sucking breathing is heard; light dimly shows* **Maggie**, *her back to us, sitting up in the 'bed'.*

Maggie   Quentin?

Quentin (*in agony*)   I'll get to it, honey.

He closes his eyes.

I'll get to it.

He stands, and as though wandering in a room he moves at random, puts a cigarette in his mouth, and strikes sparks from his lighter as darkness covers him.

Curtain.

Act Two

*The stage is dark. A spark is seen; a flame fires up. When the stage illuminates, **Quentin** is discovered lighting his cigarette – no time has passed. He continues to await the **Listener**'s return, and walks a few steps in thought and as he does a jet plane is heard, and the garbled airport announcer's voice: ' . . . from Frankfurt is now unloading at gate nine, passengers will please . . .' It becomes a watery garble and at the same moment **Holga**, beautifully dressed, walks onto the upper level with an airport porter, who leaves her bags and goes. She looks about as in a crowd – then, seeing '**Quentin**', stands on tiptoe and waves.*

Holga   Quentin! Here! Here!

She opens her arms as he evidently approaches.

Hello!

*She is gone as **Louise** rushes on from another point, a ribbon in her hair, a surgical mask hanging from her neck, a lab technician's smock open to show her sweater and long skirt of the thirties. A hospital attendant is mopping the floor behind her. She sees '**Quentin**'.*

Louise   Hello! I just got my final grades! I got an 'A' on that paper you wrote! Ya – the one on Roosevelt. I'm a Master! (*Laughs.*) And guess what Halliday said. That my style has immeasurably improved! (*Laughs; and now she walks with 'him'.*) If it wasn't for the mop I'd think you were an intern in that uniform; you look well in white. (*Her face falls; she halts.*) Oh! Then when would you be leaving? . . . No, I'm glad, I always heard Columbia Law was the best. (*Shyly.*) Actually, I could try some labs in New York, it'd be cheaper if I lived at home . . . Well, then, I'd look for something else; anyway there are more bacteriologists than bugs these days. (*With dread and shyness.*) Unless you wouldn't want me to be there. (*She bursts into an adoring smile.*) Okay! You want a malt later? I have some money, I just sold all my textbooks! Oop! (*She stops abruptly, looking down at the floor.*) I'm sorry! I forgot it was wet! See you!

With a happy wave of her hand she picks her way on tiptoe over a wet floor into darkness as a door is heard opening upstage and a light moves downstage, over the floor; **Quentin** *turns toward the returning* **Listener** *and smiles.*

Quentin   Oh, that's all right, I didn't mind waiting. How much time do I have?

He looks at his watch, coming down to the chair. **Maggie** *appears, above, in a lace wedding dress;* **Lucas**, *a designer, is on his knees finishing the vast hem.* **Carrie**, *a maid, stands by, holding gloves.* **Maggie** *is nervous, on the edge of life, looking into a 'mirror'.*

Quentin *sits in the chair. He looks forward now, to speak.*

Quentin   I, ah . . .

Lucas *gets up and quickly goes as . . .*

Maggie (*in an ecstasy of fear and hope*)   All right, Carrie, tell him to come in! (*As though trying the angular words.*) . . . My *husband!*

Carrie (*walking a few steps to a point, halts*)   You can see her now, Mister Quentin.

They are gone. He continues to the **Listener**.

Quentin   I think I can be clearer now, it shouldn't take long. I am bewildered by the death of love. And my responsibility for it.

Holga *appears again, looking about for him at the airport.*

Quentin   This woman's on my side; I have no doubt of it. And I wouldn't want to outlive another accusation. Not hers. (*He stands, agitated.*) I suddenly wonder why I risk it again. Except . . . (*Slight pause; he becomes still.*) You ever felt you once saw yourself – absolutely true? I may have dreamed it, but I swear, I feel that somewhere along the line – with Maggie I think – for one split second I saw my life; what I had done, what had been done to me, and even what I ought to do. And that vision sometimes hangs behind my head, blind now, bleached out like the moon in the morning; and if I could only let in some necessary darkness it would shine again. I think it had to do with power.

Felice *appears, about to remove the bandage.*

Quentin   Maybe that's why she sticks in my mind; she brings some darkness. Some dreadful element of power. (*He walks around her, peering . . .*) Well, that's power, isn't it? To influence a girl to change her nose, her life? . . . It does, yes, it frightens me, and I wish to God . . .

Felice (*raising her arm*)   I'll always . . .

Quentin   . . . she'd stop blessing me! (*He laughs uneasily, surprised at the force of his fear . . .*) Well, I suppose because there is a fraud involved, I have no such power.

Maggie *suddenly appears in a 'satin bed', talking into a phone.*

Maggie (*with timid idolatry*)   Hello? Is . . . How'd you know it's me? (*Laughs.*) You really remember me? Maggie? From that park that day? Well 'cause it's almost four years so I . . .

He comes away from her; she continues talking unheard. He halts near the chair. He glances toward a point where again **Felice** *appears, raising her arm in blessing, and instantly disappears, and he speaks to the* **Listener**.

Quentin   I do, yes, I see the similarity.

Laughter is heard as **Holga** *appears at a 'café table', an empty chair beside her.*

Holga   I love the way you eat! You eat like a pasha, a grand duke!

Quentin (*looks toward her, and to* **Listener**)   Yes, adored again! But . . . there is something different here.

As he moves toward **Holga**, *he says to* **Listener**:

Quentin   Now keep me to my theme. I spoke of power.

He sits beside her. As he speaks now, **Holga**'s *aspect changes; she becomes moody, doesn't face him, seems hurt. And sitting beside her he tells the* **Listener**:

Quentin   We were in a café one afternoon in Salzburg, and quite suddenly, I don't know why – it all seemed to be dying

between us. And I saw it all happening again. You know that
moment, when you begin desperately to talk about architecture?

Holga   Fifteen thirty-five. The archbishop designed it himself.

Quentin   Beautiful.

Holga (*distantly*)   Yes.

Quentin (*as though drawing on his courage, he suddenly turns to her*)
Holga. I thought I noticed your pillow was wet this morning.

Holga   It really isn't anything important.

Quentin   There are no unimportant tears. (*Takes her hand,
smiles.*) I know that much, anyway. Unless it doesn't concern
me. Is it about the concentration camp?

She wipes her eyes, unhappy with herself.

Even during the day, sometimes, you seem about to weep.

Holga   I feel sometimes . . . (*Breaks off, then:*) . . . that I'm
boring you.

Louise *appears.*

Louise   I am not all this uninteresting, Quentin!

She is gone.

Holga   I really think perhaps we've been together too much.

Quentin   Except, it's only been a few weeks.

Holga   But I may not be all that interesting.

Quentin *stares at her, trying to join this with his lost vision, and in that
mood he turns out to the* **Listener**.

Quentin   The question is power, but I've lost the connection.

Louise *appears brushing her hair.*

Quentin   Yes!

He springs up and circles **Louise**.

I tell you, there were times when she looked into the mirror and I saw she didn't like her face, and I wanted to step between her and what she saw. I felt guilty even for her face! But . . . that day . . .

He returns to the café table and slowly sits.

. . . there was some new permission . . . not to take a certain blame. There was suddenly no blame at all but that . . . we're each entitled to . . . our own unhappiness.

Holga   I wish you'd believe me, Quentin; you have no duty here.

Quentin   Holga, I would go. But the truth is, I'd be looking for you tomorrow. I wouldn't know where the hell I thought I had to be. But there's truth in what you feel. I see it very clearly; the time does come when I feel I must go. Not toward anything, or away from you. But there is some freedom in the going . . .

Mother *appears, and she is raising her arm.*

Mother   Darling, there is never a depression for great people! The first time I felt you move, I was standing on the beach at Rockaway . . .

Quentin *has gotten up from the chair, and, moving toward her:*

Quentin   But power. Where is the – ?

Mother   And I saw a star, and it got bright, and brighter, and brighter! And suddenly it fell, like some great man had died, and you were being pulled out of me to take his place, and be a light, a light in the world!

Quentin (*to* **Listener**)   Why is there some . . . air of treachery in them?

Father (*suddenly appearing – to* **Mother**)   What the hell are you talking about? We're just getting a business started again. I need him!

Quentin *avidly turns from one to the other as they argue.*

Mother   You've got Dan, you don't need him! He wants to try to get a job, go to college, maybe –

Father   He's got a job!

Mother   He means with pay! I don't want his young years going by . . . He wants a life!

Father (*indicating* **Dan**)   Why don't he 'want a life'?

Mother   Because he's different!

Father   Because *he* knows what's *right*! (*Indicating* **Mother** *and* **Quentin** *together.*) You're two of a kind – what you 'want'! Chrissake, when I was his age I was supporting six people! (*He comes up to* **Quentin**.) What are you, a stranger? *What are you?*

Quentin *is peering into the revulsion of his* **Father**'*s face. And he turns toward* **Holga** *in the café and back to* **Father**.

Quentin   Yes, I felt a power in the going . . . and treason in it . . . Because there's failure, and you turn your back on failure.

Dan   No, kid, don't feel that way. I just want to see him big again, but you go. I'll go back to school if things pick up.

Quentin (*peering at* **Dan**)   Yes, good men stay . . . although they die there.

Dan (*indicating a book in his hand*)   It's my Byron, I'll put it in your valise, and I've put in my new argyles, just don't wash them in hot water. And remember, kid, wherever you are . . .

He jumps onto a platform, calling. A passing train is heard . . .

. . . wherever you are this family's behind you! You buckle down, now . . . I'll send you a list of books to read!

Maggie (*suddenly appearing on her bed; she is addressing an empty space at the foot*)   But could I read them!

Quentin (*spins about in quick surprise*)   Huh!

All the others are gone dark but he and **Maggie**.

Maggie   I mean what kind of books? 'Cause, see . . . I never really graduated high school. (*She laughs nervously.*) Although in Social Science he liked me so he let me keep the minutes. Except I didn't know what's a minute! (*Laughs.*) I like poetry, though.

Quentin (*breaks his stare at her, and quickly comes down to the* **Listener**)   It's that I can't find myself in this vanity, any more. It's all contemptible! (*He covers his face.*)

Maggie (*enthralled, on the bed*)   I can't hardly believe you came! Can you stay five minutes? I'm a singer now, see? In fact – (*With a laugh at herself.*) I'm in the top three. And for a long time I been wanting to tell you that . . . none of it would have happened to me if I hadn't met you that day.

Quentin   . . . Yes, I see the power she offered me; but I saw beyond it once, and there was some . . . salvation in it . . . All right. I'll . . .

He turns to her, walking into her line of sight.

. . . try.

Maggie   I'm sorry if I sounded frightened on the phone but I didn't think you'd be in the office after midnight. (*Laughs at herself nervously.*) See, I only pretended to call you. Can you stay like five minutes?

Quentin (*backing into the chair*)   Sure. Don't rush.

Maggie   That's what I mean, you know I'm rushing! Would you like a drink? Or a steak? They have two freezers here. Whereas my agent went to Jamaica, so I'm just staying here this week till I go to London Friday. It's the Palladium, like a big vaudeville house, and it's kind of an honor, but I'm a little scared to go.

Quentin   Why? I've heard you; you're marvelous. Especially . . .

He can't remember a title.

Maggie   No, I'm just flapping my wings yet. I mean if you ever heard like Ella Fitzgerald or one of those . . . But did you read what that *News* fellow wrote? He keeps my records in the 'frigerator, case they melt!

Quentin (*laughs with her*) 'Little Girl Blue' – it's very moving the way you do that.

Maggie (*surprised and pleased*)   Really? 'Cause see, it's not I say to myself 'I'm going to sound sexy,' I just try to come *through* . . . like, in love or . . . (*Laughs.*) I really can't believe you're here!

Quentin   Why? I'm glad you called. I've often thought about you the last couple of years. All the great things happening to you gave me a secret satisfaction for some reason.

Maggie   Maybe 'cause you did it.

Quentin   Why do you say that?

Maggie   I don't know, just the way you looked at me . . . I didn't even have the nerve to go see an agent before that day.

Quentin   How did I look at you?

Maggie (*squinching up her shoulders, feeling for the mystery*)   Like . . . out of your *self*. See, most people they . . . just look *at* you. I can't explain it! And the way you talked to me . . .

Louise *appears.*

Louise   You think reading your brief is talking to me?

And she is gone.

Quentin (*to* **Listener**, *of* **Louise**)   Yes, I see that, but there was something more. And maybe power isn't quite the word . . .

Maggie   What did you mean . . . it gave you a secret satisfaction?

Quentin   Just that . . . like in the office, I'd hear people laughing that Maggie had the world at her feet . . .

Maggie (*hurt, mystified*)   They laughed!

Quentin   In a way.

Maggie (*in pain*)   That's what I mean; I'm a joke to most people.

Quentin   No, it's that you say what you mean, Maggie. You don't seem to be upholding anything, or . . . You're not ashamed of what you are.

Maggie   W – what do you mean of what I am?

Louise *appears; she is playing solitaire.*

Quentin (*suddenly aware he has touched a nerve*)   Well . . . that you love life, and . . . It's hard to define, I –

Louise   The word is tart. But what did it matter as long as she praised you?

Quentin (*to* **Listener**, *standing, and moving within* **Maggie**'*s area*)   But there's truth in it – I hadn't had a woman's praise, even a girl I'd laughed at with the others . . .

Maggie   But you didn't, did you?

He turns to her in agony; **Louise** *vanishes.*

Maggie   Laugh at me?

Quentin   No.

He suddenly stands and cries out to **Listener***:*

Fraud – from the first five minutes! . . . Because – I should have agreed she *was* a joke, a beautiful piece trying to take herself seriously! Why did I lie to her, play this cheap benefactor, this . . . What? (*Listens, and now, unwillingly:*) Yes, that's true too; she had a strange, surprising honor.

He turns back to her.

Maggie   Oh, hey? I just bought back two records I made!

Quentin   Bought them back how?

Maggie   Well, they're no good, just stupid rock-and-rolly stuff, and I start to think – (*Laughs shyly.*) maybe you'd **turn on** your radio, and I didn't want you to hear them. **Is that crazy?**

Quentin   No, but it's pretty unusual to care that much.

Maggie   I didn't used to, either. Honest.

Quentin (*mystified*)   But I hardly said anything to you that day.

Maggie   Well, like – (*Afraid she is silly.*) when you told me to fix where my dress was torn?

Quentin   What about it?

Maggie   You wanted me to be . . . proud of myself. Didn't you?

Quentin (*surprised*)   I guess I did, yes . . . I did.

Maggie (*feeling she has budged him*)   Would you like a drink?

Quentin (*relaxing*)   I wouldn't mind. (*Glancing around.*) What's all the flowers?

Maggie (*pouring*)   Oh, that's that dopey prince or a king or whatever he is. He keeps sending me a contract . . . whereas I get a hundred thousand dollars if we ever divorce. I'd be like a queen or something, but I only met him in El Morocco *once*! And I'm supposed to be his girl! (*She laughs, handing him his drink.*) I don't know why they print those things!

Quentin   Well, I guess everybody wants to touch you now.

Maggie   Cheers!

They drink; she makes a face.

I hate the taste but I love the effect! Would you like to take off your shoes? I mean just to rest.

Quentin   I'm okay. I thought you sounded on the phone like something frightened you.

Maggie (*evasively*)   No. I . . . You have to go home right away?

Quentin   You all alone here?

Maggie (*with a strong evasiveness*)   I don't mind that, I've always been alone. Oh, hey!

As though afraid to lose his interest, she digs into a pile of papers beside the bed, coming up with a small framed photo.

I cut your picture out of the paper last month. When you were defending that Reverend Harley Barnes in Washington? See? I framed it.

Quentin (*pleased and embarrassed*)   What'd you do that for?

Maggie   It's funny how I found it. I was on the train . . .

Quentin   Is something frightening you, Maggie?

Maggie   No, don't worry! I'm just nervous you're here. See, what I did, they kept interviewing me and asking where you were born and all, and I didn't know what to answer. Whereas my father, see, he left when I was like eighteen months, and I just thought . . . if I could see him. And maybe he would like me. Or even not. Just so he'd look. I can't explain it.

Quentin   Maybe so you'd know who you were.

Maggie   Yes! So I took the train, he's got a business upstate there, and I called him from the station. And I said, 'Can I see you?' And he said, 'Who is it?' And I said, 'It's Maggie, your daughter.' Whereas he said I wasn't from him, although my mother always said I was. And he said, 'I don't know who you are, see my lawyer.' And I told him, 'I just want you to look at me and – ' And he hung up. (*She laughs, lightly.*) So I had time and I walked around the town and I thought maybe if I could find where he eats. And I would go in, and he'd see me and maybe . . . pick me up! (*Laughs.*) 'Cause my mother said he always liked beautiful girls!

Quentin   And then you'd tell him?

Maggie   I don't know. Maybe. Maybe . . . afterwards. I don't know why I tell you that . . . Oh, yes! On the train back I found this picture in the paper. And you see the way you're looking straight in the camera? That's very hard to do, you know . . . to look absolutely straight in?

Quentin   You mean I was looking at you.

Maggie   Yes! And I said, 'I know who I am. I'm Quentin's friend.' (*Afraid she's gone too fast.*) You want another drink or . . . I mean you don't have to do anything. You don't even have to see me again.

Quentin   Why do you say that?

Maggie   'Cause I think it worries you.

Quentin   It does, yes.

Maggie   But why? I mean, can't you just be somebody's friend?

Quentin (*slight pause, and with resolve*)   Yes. I can. It's that you're so beautiful, Maggie. I don't mean only your body and your face.

Maggie (*with a sudden rush of feeling*)   I would do anything for you, Quentin. You – (*It bursts from her.*) you're like a god! S'uze me I say that but I –

Quentin (*with half a laugh*)   Maggie, anybody would have told you to mend your dress.

Maggie   No, they wouldn't.

Quentin   What then?

Maggie (*in great pain*)   Laugh. Or just . . . try for a quick one. You know.

Quentin (*to* **Listener**)   Yes! It's all so clear: the honor! The first honor was that I hadn't tried to go to bed with her! God, the hypocrisy! . . . Because, I was only afraid, and she took it for a tribute to her . . . 'value'! No wonder I can't find myself here!

He has gotten to his feet in agony.

Maggie   Oh, hey – I christened a submarine! But you know what I did?

Quentin   What?

Maggie I was voted the favorite of the Groton Shipyard!
You know, by the workers. So the Admiral handed me the
champagne bottle and I said, how come there's no workers in
the ceremony, you know? And they all laughed! So I yelled
down, and I got about ten of them to come up on the platform!
Whereas they're the ones that built it, right?

Quentin That's wonderful!

Maggie And you know what the Admiral said? I better
watch out or I'll be a Communist. Honestly! So I said, 'I don't
know what's so terrible . . . I mean they're for the poor people.'
Aren't they? The Communists?

Quentin It's a lot more complicated, honey.

Maggie But I mean, like when I was little I used to get free
shoes from the Salvation Army. Although they never fit.
(*Embarrassed, with waning conviction.*) But if the workers *do*
everything why shouldn't they have the honor? Isn't that what
you believe?

Quentin I did, yes. But the question is whether the workers
don't end up just where they are, and some new politicians on
the stand.

Maggie Oh. (*With open longing and self-loss.*) I wish I knew
something!

Quentin Honey, you know how to see it all with your own
eyes; that's more important than all the books.

Maggie But I don't know if it's true, what I see. But you do.
You see and you know if it's true.

Quentin What do you think I know?

Maggie (*some guard falling, her need rising*) Well like . . . that
I was frightened.

Quentin You frightened *now*? . . . You are, aren't you?

Maggie *stares at him in tension; a long moment passes.*

Quentin What is it, dear? You frightened to be alone here?

An involuntary half-sob escapes her. He sees she is in some great fear.

Why don't you call somebody to stay with you?

Maggie   I don't know anybody . . . like that.

Quentin (*slight pause*)   Can I do anything? Don't be afraid to ask me.

Maggie (*in a struggle she finally says*)   Would you . . . open that closet door?

Quentin (*he looks off, then back to her*)   Just open it?

Maggie   Yes.

He walks into the dark periphery; she sits up warily, watching. He returns. And she lies back.

Quentin   Do you . . . want to tell me something?

Maggie   I just never know what's right to say and I –

Quentin   Well, say it, and find out; what are people for? I'm not going to laugh. (*Sits.*) What is it?

Maggie (*with great difficulty*)   When I start to go to sleep before. And suddenly I saw smoke coming out of that closet under the door. It started to fill the whole room! (*She breaks off, near weeping.*)

Quentin (*reaches and takes her hand*)   Oh, kid, that's nothing to –

Maggie   But it kept coming and coming!

Quentin   But look – you've often dreamed such things, haven't you?

Maggie   But I was awake!

Quentin   Well, it was a waking dream. It just couldn't stay down till you went to sleep. These things can be explained if you trace them back.

Maggie   I know. I go to an analyst.

Quentin   Oh . . . then tell him about it, you'll figure it out.

Maggie   It's when I start to call you before.

She is now absorbed in her own connections.

See, my mother . . . she used to get dressed in the closet. She was very . . . like moral, you know? But sometimes she'd smoke in there. And she'd come out – you know? – with a whole cloud of smoke around her.

Quentin   Well . . . possibly you felt she didn't want you to call me.

Maggie (*astounded*)   How'd you know that?

Quentin   Because you said she was so moral. And here you're calling a married man.

Maggie   Yes! See, she tried to kill me once with a pillow on my face, whereas . . . I would turn out bad because of her . . . like her sin. And I have her hair, and the same back. (*She turns half from him, showing a naked back.*) 'Cause I have a good back, see? Every masseur says.

Quentin   Yes, it is. It's beautiful. But it's no sin to call me.

Maggie (*shaking her head like a child – with a relieved laugh at herself*)   Doesn't make me bad. Right?

Quentin   You're a very moral girl, Maggie.

Maggie (*delicately and afraid*)   W – what's moral?

Quentin   You tell the truth, even against yourself. You're not pretending to be . . . (*Turns out to the* **Listener**, *with a dread joy.*) . . . innocent! Yes, that suddenly there was someone who would not club you to death with their innocence! It's all laughable!

Felice *begins to brighten, her arms raised, just as* **Mother** *appears and she is raising her arm . . .*

Mother   I saw a star . . .

Maggie   I bless you, Quentin!

Mother *and* **Felice** *vanish as he turns back to* **Maggie**, *who takes up his photo.*

Maggie   Lot of nights when I go to sleep, I take your picture, and I bless you. You mind?

She has pressed the picture against her cheek. He bends to her, kisses her; for an instant she is unprepared, then starts to raise her arms to hold him. But he stands and backs away.

Quentin   I hope you sleep.

Maggie   I will now! (*Lies back.*) Honestly! I feel . . . all clear!

Quentin (*with a wave of his hand, backing away*)   Good luck in London.

Maggie   And . . . what's moral, again?

Quentin   To live the truth.

Maggie   That's you!

Quentin   Not yet, dear; but I intend to try.

He halts. Across the room they look at one another. He walks back to her; now he bends in and she embraces him this time, offering herself, raising her body toward him. He stands, breaking it off. And as though he knows he is taking a step . . .

Don't be afraid to call me if you need any help.

She is suddenly gone. Alone, he continues the thought.

Any time . . .

Dan *appears in crew-necked sweater with his book.*

Quentin   . . . you need anything, you call, y'hear?

Dan   This family's behind you, Quentin.

Backing into darkness, with a wave of farewell.

Any time you need anything . . .

Quentin, *surprised, has turned quickly to* **Dan**. *who disappears.*

Quentin (*to the* **Listener**, *as he still stares at the empty space* **Dan** *has left*)   You know? It isn't fraud, but some . . . disguise. I came to her like Dan . . . his goodness! No wonder I can't find myself!

Felice *appears, about to remove the 'bandage', and he grasps for the concept.*

Quentin   . . . And that girl the other night.

Felice *turns and goes.*

Quentin   When she left. It's still not clear, but suddenly those two fixtures on my wall . . .

He walks toward a 'wall', looking up.

I didn't do it, but I wanted to. Like . . .

He turns and spreads his arms in crucifixion.

. . . this!

In disgust he lowers his arms.

. . . I don't know! Because she . . . *gave* me something! She . . . let me change her! As though I – (*Cries out.*) – felt something! (*He almost laughs.*) What the hell am I trying to do, love *everybody*?

The line ends in self-contempt and anger. And suddenly, extremely fast, a woman appears in World War I costume – a Gibson Girl hat and veil over her face, ankle-length cloak, and in her hand a toy sailboat. She is bent over as though offering the boat to a little boy, and her voice is like a whisper, distant, obscure.

Mother   Quentin? Look what we brought you from Atlantic City – from the boardwalk!

The boy evidently runs away; **Mother** *instantly is anxious and angering and rushes to a point and halts, as though calling through a closed door.*

Don't lock this door! But darling, we didn't trick you, we took Dan because he's older and I wanted a rest! . . . But Fanny told you we were coming back, didn't she? Why are you running that water? Quentin, stop that water! Ike, come quick! Break down the door! Break down the door!

She has rushed off into darkness, and **Quentin** *has started after her as though to complete the memory. He halts, and speaks to the* **Listener**.

Quentin   . . . They sent me for a walk with the maid. When I came back the house was empty for a week. God, why is betrayal the only truth that sticks! . . . Yes! (*He almost laughs.*) 'Love everybody!' And I can't even mourn my own mother. It's monstrous.

The 'park bench' lights. **Maggie** *appears in a heavy, white, man's sweater, a red wig over a white angora skating cap, moccasins, and sunglasses.*

Maggie (*to the empty bench*)   Hi! It's me! (*Lifting the glasses.*) Maggie!

Quentin (*looking toward* **Maggie**)   Or mourn her, either. Is it simply grief I want? . . . No, this isn't mourning! . . . Because there's too much hatred in it!

He has come away from the adoring **Maggie** *to the chair, shaking his head.*

Quentin   . . . No, it's not that I think I killed her. It's –

An anonymous man passes **Maggie**, *glances, and goes on out.*

Maggie (*to the empty bench*)   See? I told you nobody recognizes me! Like my wig?

Quentin   . . . that I can't find myself in it, it's like another man. Only the guilt comes. Yes, or the innocence!

Maggie (*sitting beside 'him' on the bench*)   When you go to Washington tonight . . . you know what I could do? I could get on a different car on the same train!

Quentin (*to* **Listener**)   But is it enough to tell a man he is not guilty? (*Glances at her.*) My name is on this man! Why can't I say 'I'? (*Turning toward her.*) I did this. I want what I did! And I saw it once! I saw Quentin here! For one moment like the moon sees, I saw us both unblamed!

Maggie   Golly, I fell asleep the minute you left the other night! I didn't even hear you close the door! You like my wig? See? And moccasins!

Slight pause. Now he smiles.

Quentin   All you need is roller skates.

Maggie (*clapping her hands with joy*)   You're funny!

Quentin (*half to* **Listener**)   I keep forgetting . . . (*Wholly to her.*) . . . how beautiful you are. Your eyes make me shiver.

She is silent, adoring. He breaks it, sitting.

Maggie   Like to see my new apartment? There's no elevator even, or a doorman. Nobody would know. If you want to rest before you go to Washington.

He doesn't reply.

'Cause I just found out, I go to Paris after London. I'm on for two weeks, which is supposed to be unusual. But I won't be back for a while.

Quentin   How long will you be gone?

Maggie   About . . . six weeks, I think.

They both arrive at the same awareness, the separation is pain. Tears are in her eyes.

Quentin?

Quentin   Honey . . . (*Takes her hand.*) Don't look for anything more from me.

Maggie   I'm not! See, all I thought, if I went to Washington –

Quentin (*with a laugh*)   What about London?

Maggie   Oh, they'll wait. 'Cause I could register in the hotel as Miss None.

Quentin   N-u-n?

Maggie No – 'n-o-n-e' – like nothing. I made it up once, 'cause I can never remember a fake name, so I just have to think of nothing and that's me! (*She laughs with joy.*) I've done it.

Quentin It *is* a marvelous thought. The whole government's hating me, and meanwhile back at the hotel . . .

Maggie That's what I mean! Just when that committee is knocking on your head you could think of me like naked . . .

Quentin What a lovely thought.

Maggie And it would make you happy.

Quentin (*smiling warmly at her*) And nervous. But it is a lovely thought.

Maggie Because it should all be one thing, you know? Helping people, and sex. You might even argue better the next day!

Quentin (*with a new awareness, astonishment*) You know? – There's one word written on your forehead.

Maggie What?

Quentin 'Now.'

Maggie But what else is there?

Quentin A future. And I've been carrying it around all my life, like a vase that must never be dropped. So you cannot ever touch anybody, you see?

Maggie But why can't you just hold it in one hand?

He laughs.

And touch with the other! I would never bother you, Quentin.

He looks at his watch, as though beginning to calculate if there might not be time.

Can't somebody just give you something? Like when you're thirsty. And you drink, and walk away, that's all.

Quentin But what about you?

Maggie   Well . . . I would have what I gave. (*Slight pause.*)

Quentin   You're all love, aren't you?

Maggie   That's all I am! A person could die any minute, you know. (*Suddenly.*) Oh, hey! I've got a will! (*She digs into her pocket and brings out a folded sheet of notepaper.*) Could . . . I show it to you?

Quentin (*taking it*)   What do you want with a will?

Maggie   Well I'm going to do a lot of flying now and I just got my payment yesterday. Should I tell you how much?

Quentin   How much?

Maggie   Two hundred thousand dollars.

Quentin   Huh! You remember we sat right here, and I gave you five dollars?

Maggie (*with great love*)   Yes!

They stare at each other.

Really, Quentin, there's not even an elevator man.

Quentin   You want me to look at that? Honey, I've got to do one thing at a time. (*He opens the will.*)

Maggie   I understand!

He starts reading the will.

See, I'm supposed to be like a millionaire in about two years!

Laughs; he goes on reading.

Is it legal if it's not typewritten?

Quentin (*looks at her*)   Who wrote this?

Maggie   My agency; mostly Andy. Whereas he had to leave for London this morning to set everything up. And it was in a big rush.

Not comprehending, he nods and reads on.

But he's got a copy and I've got a copy.

He glances at her, bewildered.

I mean, that's what he said; that we both have copies.

He turns the page, reads on.

You got a haircut. I love the back of your head, it's sweet.

His brows knit now as he reads.

I'll shut up.

Finished reading, he stares ahead.

Or does it have to be typed?

Quentin   Who's this other signature?

Maggie   That's Jerry Moon. He's a friend of Andy in the building business, but he knows a lot about law so he signed it for a witness. I saw him sign it. In my bedroom. Isn't it good?

Quentin   It leaves everything to the agency.

Maggie   I know, but just for temporary, till I can think of somebody to put down.

Quentin   But what's all the rush?

Maggie   Well in case Andy's plane goes down. He's got five children, see, and his –

Quentin   But do you feel responsible for his family?

Maggie   Well, no. But he did help me, he loaned me money when I –

Quentin   A million dollars?

Maggie (*with a dawning awareness*)   Well, not a million. (*With fear.*) You mean I shouldn't?

Quentin   Who's your lawyer?

Two boys with bats and gloves pass, see her, walk off backward, whispering.

Maggie   Well. nobody. Jerry has a lawyer and he checks. I mean what's good for Andy's good for me, right?

Quentin (*with a certain unwillingness, even a repugnance, about interfering, he sounds neutral*)   Didn't anybody suggest you get your own lawyer?

Maggie (*with fading conviction*)   But if you trust somebody, you trust them . . . Don't you?

Quentin (*decision seizes him; he takes her hand*)   Come on, I'll walk you home.

Maggie (*standing*)   Okay! 'Cause I mean if you trust somebody!

Quentin   I'm sorry, honey, I can't advise you. Maybe you get something out of this that I don't understand. Let's go.

Maggie   No, I'm not involved with Andy. I . . . don't really sleep around with everybody, Quentin.

Quentin   Come on.

Maggie (*suddenly brightening*)   'Cause . . . I was never a prostitute. I was with a lot of men, but I never got anything. Not even for a job. I mean I'm changing. My analyst says I used to think it was like charity – sex. Like I give to those in need? (*Laughs shyly.*) Whereas I'm not an institution! Will you come in for a minute, too?

Quentin (*taking her arm*)   Sure.

A small gang of boys with baseball equipment obstructs them; one of the first pair points at her.

First Boy   It's Maggie, I told you!

Maggie (*pulling at **Quentin**'s arm, defensively*)   No, I just look like her, I'm Sarah None!

Second Boy   I can hear her voice!

Quentin   Let's go!

He tries to draw her off, but the boys grab her, and strangely she begins accepting pencils and pieces of paper to autograph.

Hey!

Crowd   How about an autograph, Maggie?

Whyn't you come down to the club?

When's your next spectacular?

Hey, Mag, I got all your records!

Sing something!

Handing over a paper for her to sign.

For my brother, Mag!

Take off your sweater, Mag, it's hot out!

How about that dance like you did on TV?

A boy wiggles sensually.

Quentin *has been thrust aside; he now reaches in, grabs her, and draws her away as she walks backward, still signing, laughing with them. The boys gone, she turns to him.*

Maggie   I'm sorry!

Quentin   It's like they're eating you. You like that?

Maggie   No, but they're just people. Could you sit down till the train? All I got so far is this French Provincial. (*Taking off her sweater.*) You like it? I picked it out myself. And my bed, and my record player. But it could be a nice apartment, couldn't it?

In silence **Quentin** *takes her hand; he draws her to him; he kisses her.*

Enflamed:

Maggie   I love you, Quentin. I would do anything for you. And I would never bother you, I swear.

Quentin   You're so beautiful it's hard to look at you.

Maggie   You didn't even see me! (*Backing away.*) Why don't you just stand there and I'll come out naked! Or isn't there a later train?

Quentin (*pause*)   Sure. There's always a later train.

He starts unbuttoning his jacket.

Maggie   I'll put music!

Quentin (*now he laughs through his words*)   Yeah, put music!

She rushes into the dark, and he strives for his moment. To the **Listener** *as he opens his jacket:*

Quentin   Here, it was somewhere here! . . . I don't know, a . . . a fraud!

A driving jazz comes on and she comes back, still dressed.

Maggie   Here, let me take off your shoes!

She drops to his feet, starting to unlace. Stiffly, with a growing horror, he looks down at her. Now shapes move in the darkness. He moves his foot away involuntarily.

Quentin   Maggie?

Maggie (*looking up from the floor, leaving off unlacing*)   Yes?

He looks around in the darkness, and suddenly his **Father** *charges forward.*

Father   What you *want*! Always what you *want*! Chrissake, what are you?

Now **Louise** *appears, reading a book, but* **Dan** *is standing beside her, almost touching her with his hand.*

Dan   This family's behind you, kid.

And **Mother**, *isolated, almost moving sensuously – and* **Quentin** *is moved, as though by them, away from* **Maggie**.

Mother   Oh, what poetry he brought me, Strauss, and novels and . . .

Quentin (*he roars out to all of them, his fists angrily in air against them*)   But where is *Quentin*?

Going toward **Mother** *in her longing:*

Yes, yes! But I know that treason! And the terror of complicity in that desire.

Turns toward **Dan**, *who has moved alongside* **Father**. *The music breaks off.*

Quentin   Yes, and to not be unworthy of those loyal, failing men! But where is Quentin? Instead of taking off my clothes, this – (*He bends to* **Maggie**, *raises her to her feet.*) posture!

Maggie   Okay. Maybe when I get back we –

Quentin   I have to say it to you, Maggie.

To **Listener***:*

Here it is, right here the killing fraud begins. (*Pause.*) You . . . have to tear up that will.

To **Listener***:*

Can't even go to bed without a principle! But how can you speak of love, she had been chewed and spat out by a long line of grinning men! Her name floating in the stench of locker rooms and parlor-car cigar smoke! She had the truth that day, I brought the lie that she had to be 'saved'! From what – except my own contempt? . . . Heh?

He is evidently caught by the **Listener***'s contradicting him, steps closer to the chair, avidly listening.*

Maggie (*to the empty space where* **Quentin** *was*)   But I showed the will to my analyst, and he said it was okay. 'Cause a person like me has to have *somebody*.

Quentin   Maggie . . . honest men don't draw wills like that.

Maggie   But it's just for temporary . . .

Quentin   Darling, if I went to Andy, and this adviser, and the analyst too, perhaps, I think they'd offer me a piece to shut up. They've got you on a table, honey, and they're carving you.

Maggie   But . . . I can't spend all that money anyway! I can't even *think* over twenty-five dollars!

Quentin   It's not the money they take, it's the dignity they destroy. You're not a piece of meat; you seem to think you owe people whatever they demand!

Maggie   I know. (*She lowers her head with a cry, trembling with hope and shame.*)

Quentin (*tilting up her face*)   But Maggie, you're somebody! You're not a kid any more running around looking for a place to sleep! It's not only your success or that you're rich – you're straight, you're serious, you're first-class, people *mean* something to you; you don't have to go begging shady people for advice like some . . . some tramp.

With a sob of love and desperation, she slides to the floor and grasps his thighs, kissing his trousers. He watches, then suddenly lifts her and, with immense pity and joy:

Maggie, stand up!

The music flies in now, and she smiles strangely through her tears, and with a kind of statement of her persisting nature begins unbuttoning her blouse, her body writhing to the beat within her clothing. And as soon as she starts her dance his head shakes . . . and to the **Listener***:*

No, not love; to stop impersonating, that's all! To live – (*Groping.*) to live in good faith if only with my guts! To . . .

Suddenly **Dan** *and* **Father** *appear together; and to them:*

Quentin   Yes! To be 'good' no more! Disguised no more! Afraid no more to show what Quentin, Quentin, Quentin . . . is!

Louise *appears, talking.*

Louise   You haven't even the decency to –

Quentin   That decency is murderous! Speak truth, not decency – I curse the whole high administration of fake innocence! I declare it, I am not innocent! Nor good!

A high tribunal dimly appears; a **Chairman** *bangs his gavel once; he is flanked by others looking down on* **Quentin** *from on high.* **Maggie** *is dropping her blouse.*

Chairman   But really Reverend Barnes cannot object to answering whether he attended the Communist-run Peace Congress in Prague, Czechoslovakia. No – no, counsel will not be allowed to confer with the witness, this is not a trial! Any innocent man would be . . .

Quentin   And this question – innocent! How many Negroes you allow to vote in your patriotic district? And which of your social, political, or racial sentiments would Hitler have disapproved? And not a trial? You fraud, your 'investigators' this moment are working this man's church to hound him out of it!

Harley Barnes (*appears rising to his feet; he has a clerical collar*) I decline on the grounds of the First and Fifth Amendments to the Constitution.

Quentin (*with intense sorrow*)   But are we sure, Harley – I ask it, I ask it – if the tables were turned, and they were in front of you would you permit *them* not to answer? Hateful men that they are?

Harley *looks at him indignantly, suspiciously.*

Quentin   I am not sure what we are upholding any more – are we good by merely saying no to evil? Even in a righteous 'no' there's some disguise. Isn't it necessary . . . to say . . .

Harley *is gone, and the tribunal.* **Maggie** *is there, snapping her fingers, letting down her hair.*

Quentin   . . . to finally say yes . . . to *something*?

A smile of pain and longing has come into his face, and **Maggie** *expands now, slipping out of her skirt, dancing in place. He goes to her and grasps her body, moving with her serpentine motion.*

Quentin   A fact . . . a fact . . . a thing.

Maggie *embraces him and then lies down on the 'bed' with the imagined* **Quentin**.

Maggie   Sing inside me.

Quentin *moves to the chair facing the* **Listener**; *she continues on the bed behind him as he sits.*

Quentin   Even condemned, unspeakable like all truth!

Maggie   Become happy.

Quentin (*still to the* **Listener**)   Contemptible like all truth.

Maggie   That's all I am.

Quentin   Covered like truth with slime; blind, ignorant.

Maggie   But nobody ever said to me, stand up!

Quentin   The blood's fact, the world's blind gut . . . yes!

Maggie   Now.

Quentin   To this, yes.

Maggie   Now . . . now.

Her recorded number ends and only the thumping needle in the empty groove is heard through the lengthening darkness. Then her voice, pillowed and soft.

Maggie   Quentin?

Light finds her prone on a bed, alone on the stage, a sheet partly covering her naked body. Her chin rests languidly on her hands. She glances toward a point, off.

Quenny? That soap is odorless, so you don't have to worry.

Slight pause.

It's okay! Don't rush; I love to wait for you!

Her eye falls on his shoe on the floor. She picks it up, strokes it.

I love your shoes. You have good taste!

Slight pause.

S'uze me I didn't have anything for you to eat, but I didn't know! I'll get eggs, though, case maybe in the mornings. And steaks – case at night. I mean just in case. You could have it just the way you want, just any time.

Quentin *stands looking front; she speaks to empty space from the bed.*

Maggie   Like me?

He glances back at her adoring face, as **Holga** *appears above in the airport, looking about for him.* **Maggie** *remains on the bed, stroking his shoe.*

Quentin (*glancing at* **Maggie**)   It's all true, but it isn't the truth. I know it because it all comes back too cheap; my bitterness is making me lie. I'm afraid. To make a promise. Because I don't know who'll be making it. I'm a stranger to my life.

Maggie (*she has lifted a tie off the floor*)   Oh, your tie got all wrinkled! I'm sorry! But hey, I have a tie! (*Jumping up with the sheet around her.*) It's beautiful, a regular man's tie – (*Catching herself.*) I . . . just happen to have it!

She tries to laugh it off and goes into darkness. **Holga** *is gone.*

Quentin   I tell you, below this fog of tawdriness and vanity, there is a law in this disaster, and I saw it once as hard and clear as a statute. But I think I saw it . . . with some love. Or simply wonder, but not blame. It's . . . like my mother; so many of my thoughts of her degenerate into some crime; the truth is she was a light to me whenever it was dark. I loved that nut, and only love does make her real and mine. Or can one ever remember love? It's like trying to summon up the smell of roses in a cellar. You might see a rose, but never the perfume. And that's the truth of roses, isn't it – the perfume?

Maggie *appears in light in a wedding dress;* **Carrie**, *the maid, is just placing a veiled hat on her head;* **Lucas**, *the designer, is on his knees hurriedly fixing the last hem.* **Maggie** *is turning herself wide-eyed in a mirror.* **Quentin** *begins to rise.*

Maggie   Okay! Let him in, Carrie! Thanks, Lucas, but I don't want him to wait any more, the ceremony is for three! Hurry, please!

Lucas *sews faster;* **Carrie** *goes to a point, calls down.*

Carrie   Mister Quentin? You can see her now.

Quentin   I want to see her with . . . that love again! Why is it so hard? Standing there, that wishing girl, that victory in lace.

We had turned all mockery to purpose, and purpose moved around us like the natural shadows of the day!

Maggie (*looking ahead on the edge of life as* **Lucas** *bites off the last threads*) You won't hardly know me any more, Lucas! He saved me, I mean it! I've got a new will and I even changed my analyst, I've got a wonderful doctor now! And we're going to do all my contracts over, which I never got properly paid. And Ludwig Reiner's taking me! And he won't take even opera singers unless they're, you know, like artists! No matter how much you want to pay him. I didn't even dare but Quentin made me go – and now he took me, imagine! Ludwig Reiner!

She turns, seeing **Quentin** *entering. An awe of the moment takes them both;* **Lucas** *goes.* **Carrie** *lightly touches* **Maggie**'s *forehead and silently prays, and walks off.*

Quentin   Oh, my darling. How perfect you are.

Maggie   Like me?

Quentin   Good God – to come home every night – to *you*!

He starts for her open-armed, laughing, but she touches his chest, excited and strangely fearful.

Maggie   You still don't have to do it, Quentin. I could just come to you whenever you want.

Quentin (*it hurts him but he tries to laugh again*)   You just can't believe in something good really happening. But it's real, darling, you're my wife!

Maggie (*with a hush of fear on her voice*)   I want to tell you something.

Quentin   I know enough. Come.

Maggie (*slipping her hand out of his*)   I just want to tell you!

Quentin   Darling, you're always making new revelations, but that stuff doesn't matter any more.

Maggie (*pleased, and like a child wanting some final embrace*)   But the reason I went into analysis! I never told you *that*!

Quentin (*smiling above his own foreboding*)   All right, what?

Maggie   'Cause you said we have to love what happened, didn't you? Even the bad things?

Quentin (*seriously now, to match her intensity*)   Yes, I did.

Maggie   I . . . was with two men . . . the same day. (*She has turned her eyes from him.*) I mean the same day, see. But I didn't realize it till that night. And I got very scared. (*She almost weeps now, and looks at him, subservient and oddly chastened.*) I'll always love you, Quentin. But don't be afraid what people say, we could just tell them we changed our mind, and get in the car and maybe go to a motel . . .

Anonymous men appear in the farthest distance and vanish as **Quentin** *shakes his head.*

Quentin   Look, darling. It wasn't you . . . (*Reaching for her hand again.*) Come now.

Maggie   But maybe in a way it was. In a way! I don't know!

Quentin   Sweetheart, everyone does things that . . .

To **Listener***, with sudden realization:*

Quentin   Here, here is part of it! One part is that . . .

Back to her:

An event itself, dear, is not important; it's what you took from it. Whatever happened to you, this is what you made of it and I love this.

To **Listener***, rapidly:*

. . . Yes! That we conspired to violate the past, and the past is holy and its horrors are holiest of all!

Turning back to **Maggie***.*

And . . . something . . . more . . .

Maggie (*with hope now*)   Maybe . . . it would even make me a better wife, right?

Quentin (*with hope against the pain*)   That's the way to talk!

Maggie (*with gladness, seeing a fruit of the horror*)   'Cause I'm not curious! You be surprised, a lot of women, they smile and their husbands never know, but they're curious. But I *know* – I have a king, and *I know*!

A wedding march strikes up. It shatters her fragile vision; he takes her arm.

There's people who . . . going to laugh at you.

Quentin   Not any more, dear, they're going to see what I see. Come!

Maggie (*not moving with him*)   What do you see? Tell me! (*Bursting out of her.*) 'Cause I . . . you were ashamed once, weren't you?

Quentin   I see you suffering, Maggie; and once I saw it, all shame fell away.

Maggie   You . . . were ashamed!?

Quentin (*with difficulty*)   Yes. But you're a victory, Maggie, for yourself and me. And somehow for everyone. (*He kisses her hand.*) Believe it, darling, you're like a flag to me, a kind of proof, somehow, that people can win.

Maggie   And you . . . you won't ever look at any other woman, right?

Quentin   Darling, a wife can be loved! You never saw it but . . .

Maggie (*with a new intensity of conflict*)   Before, though – why did you kiss that Elsie?

Quentin   Just hello. She always throws her arms around people.

Maggie   But . . . why's you let her rub her body against you?

Quentin (*laughs*)   She wasn't rubbing her . . .

Maggie (*downing a much greater anxiety*)   I saw it. And you stood there.

Quentin (*trying to laugh*)   Maggie, it was a meaningless gesture.

Maggie   But you told me yourself that I have to look for the meaning of things, didn't you? You want me to be like I used to be? Like nothing means anything, it's all a fog? (*Now pleadingly, and vaguely wronged.*) I'm just trying to understand; you mustn't laugh. Why did you let her do that?

Quentin   She came up to me and threw her arms around me, what could I do?

Maggie (*a flash of contemptuous anger*)   What do you mean? You just tell her to knock it off!

Quentin (*taken aback*)   I . . . don't think you want to sound like this, honey.

Maggie (*frightened she has shown a forbidden side*)   Sound like what?

Quentin (*trying to brush it away*)   Darling, you're just frightened and it magnifies every threat. Come, they're waiting.

He puts her arm in his; they turn to go.

Maggie (*almost in tears*)   Teach me, Quentin! I don't know how to be!

Quentin   Yes, darling. Now we start to be. Both of us.

They begin moving in processional manner toward a group of guests.

Maggie   It's that nobody's here . . . from me. I'm like a stranger here! If my mother or my father or anybody who loved me –

Quentin   Be calm, dear, everyone here adores you.

*Now as **Maggie** speaks she continues in processional tread, but he remains behind, staring at her; and she goes on with 'him', her arm still held as before, but in midair now.*

Maggie   I'm sorry if I sounded that way, but you want me to say what I feel, don't you? See, till you, I never said anything, Quentin; you like gave me my feelings to say! You don't want me just smiling, like most women, do you?

During her speech **Louise** *has appeared.*

Quentin (*as against the vision of* **Louise**)   No. *Say* what you feel; the truth is on our side; always say it!

Louise *is gone.*

Maggie (*faltering, but going on*)   You're not holding me!

Quentin (*half the stage away now, and turning toward the empty air*) I am, darling, I'm with you!

Maggie (*as she walks into darkness*)   I'm going to be a good wife, I'm going to be a good wife . . . Quentin, I don't feel it!

Quentin (*both frustrated and with an appeal to her*)   I'm holding you! See everybody smiling, adoring you? Look at the orchestra guys making a V for victory! Everyone loves you, darling! Why are you sad?

Suddenly, the 'Wedding March' is gone as from the far depths of the stage, her shape undefined, she calls out with a laugh.

Maggie   Surprise! You like it? They rushed it while we were away!

Quentin (*slight pause; they are half a stage apart*)   Yes, it's beautiful!

The dialogue is now condensed, like time swiftly passing in the mind.

Maggie   See how large it makes the living room? And I want to take down that other wall too! Okay?

Quentin (*not facing her direction; to his memory of it*)   But we just finished putting those walls in.

Maggie   Well it's only money; I want it big, like a castle for you! You want it beautiful, don't you?

Quentin   It's lovely, dear, but . . . maybe wait till next year with the other wall. We're behind in the taxes, darling.

Maggie   But we could die tomorrow! Used to say, I have one word written on my forehead – why can't it be beautiful now? I get all that money next year.

Quentin   But see, dear, you owe almost all of it . . .

Maggie   Quentin, don't hold the future like a vase – touch now, touch me! I'm here, and it's now!

Quentin   Okay! Tear it down! Make it beautiful! Do it now! Maybe I *am* too cautious. Forgive me.

Her voice is suddenly heard in a vocal number. He breaks into a genuine smile of joy.

Maggie, sweetheart – that's magnificent!

Now she appears, in blouse, leotards, high heels, listening and pacing. Several executives in dark suits appear, listening carefully.

Maggie   No! Tell me the truth! That piano's off, you're not listening!

Quentin   But nobody'll ever notice that.

A pianist moves near her out of the executive group.

Maggie   I know the difference! Don't you want me to be good? I *told* Weinstein I wanted Johnny Block but they give me this fag and he holds back my beat! Nobody listens to me, I'm a joke!

Quentin   All right, dear, maybe if I talked to Weinstein –

Maggie   No, don't get mixed up in my crummy business, you've got an important case . . .

Quentin (*he moves to a point and demands*)   Weinstein, get her Johnny Block!

The music turns over into another number and her voice, swift, sure.

There now! Listen now!

She listens in suspense; he almost struts with his power.

See? There's no reason to get upset, just tell me and I'll talk to these people any time you –

Maggie   Oh, thank you, darling! See? They respect you. Ask Ludwig, soon as you come in the studio my voice flies! Oh, I'm going to be a good wife, Quentin, I just get nervous sometimes that I'm – (*She sits as the music goes out.*) – only bringing you my problems. But I want my stuff to be perfect, and all they care is if they can get rich on it.

The executives are gone.

Quentin   Exactly, dear – so how can you look to them for your self-respect? Come, why don't we go out for a walk? We never walk any more. (*He sits on his heels beside her.*)

Maggie   You love me?

Quentin   I adore you. I just wish you could find some joy in your life.

Maggie   Quentin, I'm a joke that brings in money.

Quentin   I think it's starting to change, though – you've got a great band now, and Johnny Block, and the best sound crew . . .

Maggie   Only because I fought for it. You'd think somebody'd come to me and say, Look, Maggie, you made us all this money, now we want you to develop yourself, what can we do for you?

Quentin   Darling, they'd be selling frankfurters if there were more money in it, how can you look to them for love?

Maggie (*alone, alone*)   But where will I look?

Quentin (*thrown down*)   Maggie, how can you say that?

Maggie (*she stands; there is an underlying suspiciousness now*)   When I walked into the party you didn't even put your arms around me. I felt like one of those *wives* or something!

Quentin   Well, Donaldson was in the middle of a sentence and I –

Maggie   So what? *I walked into the room!* I hire him, he doesn't hire me!

Quentin   But he is directing your TV show and I was being polite to him.

Maggie   You don't have to be ashamed of me, Quentin. I had a right to tell him to stop those faggy jokes at my rehearsal. Just because he's cultured? I'm the one the public pays for, not Donaldson! Ask Ludwig Reiner what my value is!

Quentin   I married you, Maggie, I don't need Ludwig's lecture on your value.

Maggie (*looking at him with strange eyes – with a strange laugh*) Why . . . why you so cold?

Quentin   I'm not cold, I'm trying to explain what happened.

Maggie   Well, take me in your arms, don't explain.

He takes her in his arms, kisses her, and she plaintively instructs.

Not like that. *Hold* me.

Quentin (*he tries to hold her tighter, then releases her*)   Let's go for a walk, honey. Come on . . .

Maggie (*sinking*)   What's the matter?

Louise *appears, playing solitaire.*

Quentin   Nothing.

Maggie   But Quentin . . . you should look at me more. I mean . . . like I *existed* or something. Like you used to look – out of your *self.*

Louise *vanishes.* **Maggie** *moves away into darkness, deeply discouraged.*

Quentin (*alone*)   I adore you, Maggie; I'm sorry; it won't ever happen again. Never! You need more love than I thought. But I've got it, and I'll make you see it, and when you do you're going to astound the world!

A rose light floods a screen; **Maggie** *emerges in a dressing gown, indicating an unseen window.*

Maggie   Surprise! You like it? See the material?

Quentin   Oh, that's lovely! How'd you think of that?

Maggie   All you gotta do is close them and the sun makes the bed all rose.

Quentin (*striving for joy*)   Yes, it's beautiful! You see? An argument doesn't mean disaster! Oh, Maggie, I never knew what love was!

Takes her in his arms.

Maggie (*her spirit gradually falling*)   'Case during the day, like maybe you get the idea to come home and we make love again in daytime. (*She ends sitting in a weakness; nostalgically:*) Like last year, remember? In the winter afternoons? And once there was still snow on your hair. See, that's all I am, Quentin.

Quentin   I'll come home tomorrow afternoon.

Maggie   Well don't *plan* it.

He laughs, but she looks at him; her stare is piercing. His laugh dies.

Quentin   What is it? See, I don't want to hide things any more, darling. The truth saves, always remember that – tell me, what's bothering you?

Maggie (*shaking her head, seeing*)   I'm not a good wife. I take up so much of your work.

Quentin   No, dear. I only said that because you – (*Striving, against his true resentment.*) – you kind of implied that I didn't fight the network hard enough on that penalty, and I got it down to twenty thousand dollars. They had a right to a hundred when you didn't perform.

Maggie (*with rising indignation*)   But can't I be sick? I was sick!

Quentin   I know, dear, but the doctor wouldn't sign the affidavit.

Maggie (*furious at him*)   I had a pain in my side, for Christ's sake, I couldn't stand straight! You don't believe me, do you!

Quentin   Maggie, I'm only telling you the legal situation.

Maggie   Ask Ludwig what you should do! You should've gone in there roaring! 'Stead of a polite liberal and affidavits and –

Quentin (*hurt*)   Don't say that, Maggie.

Maggie   Well, ask him! You don't know what a star's rights are! I make millions for those people!

Quentin   Maggie, I always thought I was a pretty good lawyer . . .

Maggie   I'm not saying Ludwig is a lawyer.

Quentin   I know, dear, but he's always got these brave solutions but the two-three times I've tried to pin him down to specifics he gets full of oxygen.

Maggie   Now you're hurt! I can't *say* anything!

Quentin   Well, honey, I'm putting in forty per cent of my time on your problems.

Maggie   You are not putting –

Quentin (*horrified she doesn't know – an outburst*)   Maggie, I keep a log; I know what I spend my time on!

She looks at him, shaking her head; mortally wounded, tears in her eyes. She goes to a bottle and pours.

I'm sorry, darling, but when you talk like that I feel a little . . . like a fool. Don't start drinking; please.

She drinks.

Look, I don't object to the time I spend, I'm happy to do it, but –

Maggie   Should never gotten married. I knew it. Soon's they got married it all changes. Every man I ever knew they hate their wives.

Quentin   Honey, it always comes down to the same thing, don't you see? Now listen to me. (*Turns her.*) You're still proceeding on the basis that you're alone. That you can be disposed of. And the slightest contradiction of your wishes makes the earth tremble. But –

Maggie   You taught me to speak out, Quentin, and when I do you get mad.

Quentin   I'm not mad, I'm frustrated that you can't seem to pick up the joy we could have. My greatest happiness is when I know I've helped to make you smile, to make you –

Maggie   But the only reason I went to see Ludwig was so you'd be proud of me, so you could say, 'See? I found her, she was a little lost nut, and look, look what became of Maggie!' It's all for you, that's why I want it good!

Quentin   Then what are we arguing about? We want the same thing, you see?

Suddenly to **Listener**:

Power! Yes, the power, the power to . . . to . . . Wait a minute, I had it, and I lost it.

Maggie (*pouring another drink*)   So maybe the best thing is if I get a lawyer . . . you know, just a stranger.

Quentin (*slight pause; hurt*)   Okay.

Maggie   It's nothing against you; but see, like that girl in the orchestra, that cellist – I mean, Andy took too much but he'd have gone in there and got rid of her. I mean, you don't laugh when a singer goes off key.

Quentin   But she said she coughed.

Maggie (*furiously*)   She didn't cough, she laughed! And you stand there going ho-ho-ho to her high-class jokes! Christ sake, just because she played in a symphony?

Quentin   Maggie, I stopped by to pick you up, I said hello to her and –

Maggie   I'm not finishing this tape if she's in the band tomorrow! I'm entitled to my conditions, Quentin! (*Commanding.*) And I don't have to plead with anybody! I want her out!

Quentin (*quietly*)   All right. I'll call Weinstein in the morning.

Maggie   You won't. You're too polite.

Quentin   I've done it before, Maggie; three others in three different bands.

Maggie   Well, so what? You're my husband. You're supposed to do that. Aren't you?

Quentin   But I can't pretend to enjoy demanding people be fired.

Maggie   But if it was your daughter you'd get angry, wouldn't you? Instead of apologizing for her?

Quentin (*envisions it*)   I guess I would, yes. I'm sorry. I'll do it in the morning.

Maggie (*with desperate warmth*)   That's all I mean. If I want something you should ask yourself why, why does she want it, not why she shouldn't have it. That's why I don't smile, I feel I'm fighting all the time to make you *see*. You're like a little boy, you don't see the knives people hide.

Quentin   I see the knives, but . . . It's the same thing again. You still don't believe you're not alone.

Maggie   Then make me believe it!

Quentin   I'm trying, darling, but sometimes you say a thing that cuts me down like a . . . Maggie, I'm not cold to you.

Maggie   I didn't mean you're cold. It's just . . . I've seen such terrible things, Quentin. I never told you most of it. And when you're alone all you have is what you can see. Ask my doctor – I see more than most people, 'cause I had to protect myself.

Quentin   But sweetheart, that's all gone. You've got a husband now who loves you.

Pause. She seems to fear greatly.

Maggie   But it's not all gone. When your mother tells me I'm getting fat, I know where I am – and when you don't do anything about it.

Quentin   But what can I do?

Maggie   Slap her down, that's what you do!

Quentin   But she says anything comes into her head, dear.

Maggie   She insulted me! She's jealous of me!

Quentin   Maggie, she adores you.

Maggie   What are you trying to make me think, I'm crazy?

Quentin   Why does everything come down to –

Maggie   I'm not crazy!

Quentin (*carefully, on eggs*)   The thought never entered my mind, darling. I'll . . . talk to her.

Maggie (*mimicking him as though he were weak*)   'I'll talk to her.' She hates me!

Quentin   I'll tell her to apologize.

Maggie   But at least get a little angry!

Quentin   All right, I'll do it.

She drinks.

Maggie   I'm not going to work tomorrow.

She lies down on the 'bed' as though crushed.

Quentin   Okay.

Maggie (*half springing up*)   You know it's not 'okay'! You're scared to death they'll sue me, why don't you say it?

Quentin   I'm not scared to death; it's just that you're so wonderful in this show and it's a pity to –

Maggie (*sitting up furiously*)   All you care about is money! Don't shit me!

The anonymous men appear in the distance.

Quentin (*quelling a fury – his voice very level*) Maggie, don't use that language with me, will you?

Maggie Calling me vulgar, that I talk like a truck driver! Well, that's where I come from. I'm for Negroes and Puerto Ricans and truck drivers!

Quentin Then why do you fire people so easily?

Maggie (*her eyes narrowing, she is seeing him anew*) Look. You don't want me. What the hell are you doing here?

Quentin (*with a quavering, mountainous restraint*) I live here. And you do too, but you don't know it yet. But you're going to. I . . .

Father *appears.*

Father Where's he going, I need him! What are you?

And he is gone.

Quentin I'm here, and I stick it. And one day you're going to catch on. Now go to sleep, I'll be back in ten minutes, I'd like to take a walk.

He starts out and she comes to attention.

Maggie Where you going to walk?

Quentin Just around the block.

She watches him carefully. He sees her suspicion.

There's nobody else, kid; I just want to walk.

Maggie (*with great suspicion*) 'Kay.

He goes a few yards, halts, turns to see her taking a pill bottle and unscrewing the top.

Quentin (*coming back*) You can't take pills on top of whiskey, dear.

He has reached for them; she pulls them away but he grabs them again and puts them in his pocket.

That's how it happened the last time. And it's not going to happen again. Never. I'll be right back.

Maggie (*she pours again*)   Why you wear those pants?

He turns back to her, knowing what is coming.

I told you the seat is too tight.

Quentin   Well, they made them too tight, but I can take a walk in them.

Maggie   Fags wear pants like that; I told you.

She drinks again. It is so pathological he looks with amazed eyes.

They attract each other with their asses.

Quentin   You calling me a fag now?

Maggie (*she is very drunk*)   Just I've known fags and some of them didn't even know themselves that they were. And I didn't know if you knew about that.

Quentin   That's a hell of a way to reassure yourself, Maggie.

Maggie (*staggering slightly*)   I'm allowed to say what I see . . .

Quentin   You trying to get me to throw you out? Is that what it is? So it'll get real?

Maggie (*pointing at him, at his control*)   Wha's that suppose to be, strong and silent? I mean what is it?

She stumbles and falls. He makes no move to pick her up.

Quentin (*standing over her, quite knowing she is beyond understanding*) And now I walk out, huh? And it's real again, huh?

He picks her up angrily.

Is that what you want?

Maggie (*breaking from him*)   I mean what *is* it?

She pitches forward; he catches her and roughly puts her on the bed.

Wha's the angle? I mean what is it?

She gets on her feet again.

You gonna wait till I'm old? You know what another cab driver said to me today? 'I'll give you fifty dollars.'

An open sob, wild and contradictory, flies out of her.

You know what's fifty dollars to a cab driver?

Her pain moves into him, his anger is swamped with it.

Go ahead, you can go; I can even walk a straight line, see? Look, see?

She walks with arms out, one foot in front of the other.

So what is it, heh? I mean what is it? I mean you want dancing? You want dancing?

Quentin   Please don't do that.

Breathlessly she turns on the phonograph and goes into a hip-flinging, broken-ankle step around him.

Maggie   I mean what do you want! What is it?

He hasn't been looking at her, but beyond her, and now she starts tumbling about and he catches her and lays her down on the bed.

I mean, you gonna wait till I'm old? Or what? I mean what is it?

She lies there gasping. He stares down at her, addressing the **Listener**.

Quentin   That there is a love; limitless; a love not even of persons but blind, blind to insult, blind to the spear in the flesh, like justice blind, like . . .

Felice *appears.* **Quentin** *slowly raises up his arms; holds them there. But his face is drawn together in his quest.* **Maggie** *speaks from the bed, half-asleep.*

Maggie   Hey? Why?

Felice *vanishes. He lowers his arms, peering for his answer, as . . .*

Maggie   I mean what do you want? Whyn't you beat it? I mean what is it?

Father *appears.*

Father   What are . . .

Quentin *shakes his head, an unformed word of negation in his mouth.*

Dan *appears.*

Dan   This family is always behind you, boy; anything you need, just . . .

Mickey *appears.* **Quentin** *moves toward him.*

Mickey   . . . That we both go back, Lou, you and I together; and name the names.

Quentin (*shaking the vision out of his head as false and crying out as* **Dan** *and* **Father** *disappear*)   No! I had it! In whose name you turn your back! I saw it clear! I saw the name!

Lou *appears on high; the approaching sound of a subway train is heard and he seems to fall off a platform to the wracking squeal of brakes, crying:*

Lou   Quentin!

He is gone, and **Mickey** *is gone.* **Quentin**'s *hands are a vise against his head. The tower lights as . . .*

Quentin (*on new level of angry terror*)   In whose name? In whose blood-covered name do you look into a face you loved, and say, Now, you have been found wanting, and now in your extremity you die! It had a name, it . . .

Behind his back, in the farthest extremity of the stage, hardly visible excepting as a bent-over shape, **Mother** *appears in pre-World War I costume, calling in a strange whisper:*

Mother   Quentin? Quentin?

She is moving rapidly through shadow. He hurries toward her, but in fear.

Quentin   Hah? Hah?

Mother   See what we brought you from Atlantic City! From the boardwalk!

A tremendous crash of surf spins him about, and **Mother** *is gone and the light of the moon is rising on the pier.*

Quentin   . . . By the ocean. That cottage. That last night.

Maggie *in a rumpled wrapper, a bottle in her hand, her hair in snags over her face, staggers out to the edge of the 'pier' and stands in the sound of the surf. Now she starts to topple over the edge of the 'pier' and he rushes to her and holds her in his hands. She slowly turns around and sees it's he. Now the sound of jazz from within is heard, softly.*

Maggie   You were loved, Quentin; no man was ever loved like you.

Quentin (*releasing her*)   Carrie tell you I called? My plane couldn't take off all day . . .

Maggie (*drunk, but aware*)   I was going to kill myself just now. (*She walks past him. He is silent. She turns.*) Or don't you believe that either?

Quentin (*with an absolute calm, a distance, but without hostility*) I saved you twice, why shouldn't I believe it? (*Going toward her.*) This dampness is bad for your throat, you oughtn't be out here.

Maggie (*she defiantly sits, her legs dangling*)   Where've *you* been?

Quentin   I've been in Chicago. I told you. The Hathaway estate.

Maggie (*a sneer*)   Estates!

Quentin   Well, I have to make a living before I save the world.

He goes into the bedroom, removing his jacket.

Maggie (*from the pier*)   Didn't you hear what I told you?

Quentin   I heard it. I'm not coming out there, Maggie, it's too wet.

She looks out a moment, wide-eyed at the neutrality of his tone; then gets up and unsteadily comes into the room. He is taking off his tie.

Maggie   What's *this* all about?

Quentin   Just going to sleep. I'm very tired. I don't feel too hot.

Maggie   Tired.

Quentin   Yep. I can get tired too.

Maggie   Poor man.

Quentin   Not any more, no.

He sits on the bed unlacing his shoes. Sensing, she sits on a chair, the pill bottle in her hand.

Maggie (*like a challenge to him*)   I didn't go to rehearsal today.

Quentin   I didn't think you did.

Maggie   I called Weinstein; I'm not working on his label any more and I don't care if he's got ten contracts. And I called the network; I'm not doing that stupid show, and I don't owe it to them regardless of any promise you made me make. I'm an artist and I don't have to do stupid shows no matter what contract!

Quentin   Maggie, I'm not your lawyer any more; tell it to –

Maggie   I told him. And he's getting me out of both contracts. And no arguments either.

Quentin   Good. I'll sleep in the living room. I've got to rest.

He starts out.

Maggie (*holding up the bottle*)   Here, count them if you want to, I only took a few.

Quentin   I'm not counting pills any more, Maggie, I've given up being the policeman. But if you want to, I wish you'd tell me how many you had before I came. 'Cause they should know that in case they have to pump you out tonight.

Maggie (*hurt and bewildered*)   What is this?

Quentin   Just that I can't pull on the other end of that rope any more. And I see the signs, honey, so I'm telling you in advance. The last two times when we got you out of it you thanked me for saving your life, and for days everything was warm and sweet. I'm not your analyst, but if this is how you create a happy reunion, forget it – this time I call the ambulance, so if you do wake up it'll be in the hospital, and that means the newspapers. I'm just trying to remove one of the motives, if a happy reunion is one of them – because I'm not going to be the rescuer any more. It's only fair to tell you, I just haven't got it any more. They're your pills and your life; you keep the count.

He starts out.

Maggie   What . . . what's all this? Well, don't run away like a kid. What is all this?

Quentin (*halts; a pause*)   Well . . . one thing is that I've been fired. And that's what I've been doing in Chicago. Max is there and I went to convince him that I oughtn't be let out of the firm.

Maggie   You're not fired.

Quentin   In fact, it's the second time in six months. I can't make a decision any more without something sits up inside me and busts out laughing.

Maggie   That my fault, heh?

Quentin   Maggie, I only tell it to you so you'll understand that the question is no longer whether you'll survive, but also whether I will. Because I'm backed up to the edge of the cliff, and I haven't one inch left behind me. And that's the difference tonight, Maggie. So take care what you ask me, dear, because all I've got left is the truth. You know that feeling?

They hold each other's gaze. She unscrews the bottle and takes out a pill and swallows it.

Okay.

He sits on the bed, and puts his shoes on again.

Maggie   What are you doing?

Quentin   I'll sleep at the inn tonight. I think you're safer without me here. I think I've turned into some kind of ogre to you; and I haven't the strength to try to correct it any more.

He gets his tie.

Maggie (*her speech thicker, but she is doped rather than drunk*) Don't . . . do that.

He looks at her lost face.

Please. Please . . . sit down.

And as she did when they first met, but in a caricature of that invitingness, she indicates a chair.

Could you . . . just while I . . . go to sleep? Please?

Quentin (*gently moved*)   Okay, if you lie down and go to sleep.

Maggie   I'll . . . lie down here. See? (*She quickly goes to the bed, clutching her pills, and lies down.*) See?

He sits facing her, a yard away. Silence.

'Member? How used talk to me till I fell asleep?

Quentin   I've sat beside you for days and weeks at a time, Maggie, but you never remember. I've taken you for long drives to soothe you; sailed you around the bay for hours and my office looking high and low for me, but all you remember is the bad.

Maggie   Could you stay . . . like five minutes?

Quentin (*pause; he tries not to weep*)   Yes.

Maggie (*slight pause; suddenly she puts the pills on the floor*)   See? I'm not taking any more.

He is silent.

I only had . . . about fifteen, I think. You . . . you can have the bottle if you want, even.

Quentin (*without rancor; explaining*)   I don't want the bottle; I'm not the policeman any more.

Maggie   Please don't call the ambulance.

Quentin   Then don't take any more. I just can't go through it alone again, and I'm telling you.

Maggie (*slight pause*)   You going back to your former wife, right?

Quentin   No, I've . . . *been* there.

Maggie   What then?

Quentin (*long pause*)   Well, the first thing I've got to do is . . . get somebody to take care of you.

Maggie (*very carefully*)   What do you mean, take care of me?

Quentin (*pause; under terrific stress he begins to touch his face, then puts his hand down*)   I talked to your doctor this afternoon.

Maggie (*the terror growing*)   About what? Thought you said your plane didn't take off.

Quentin   I was lying again, but there's no point to it any more. I just didn't want to have this conversation when you –

Maggie   I hear everything; what'd you talk to my doctor about? You going to put me somewhere? Is that it?

Quentin   No. But you should be supervised. And I shouldn't be with you any more. I shouldn't have been for at least a year, in fact.

Maggie   Well now you got what you wanted, didn't you.

Quentin   No, exactly the opposite. But he's trying to get a plane up here; if he can he'll spend the night with you; and you can decide with him what to do. But we shouldn't argue any more. It's between you and him.

Maggie (*with a knowing, determined smile*)   You're not going to put *me* anywhere, mister.

Quentin   I've nothing to do with that, Maggie, it's you and him.

Maggie   Why, what'd you say to him?

Quentin   Maggie, you want to die and I don't know any more how to prevent it. Maybe it was just my being out in the real world for twenty-four hours again, but it struck me that I'm playing with your life out of some idiotic hope of some kind that you're suddenly going to come out of this endless spell. I think somebody ought to be with you who has no illusions of that kind, and simply watches constantly to prevent it.

Maggie   Maybe a little love would prevent it.

Quentin   But how would you know, Maggie? Not that I love you, but if I did, would you know any more? Do you know who I am? Aside from my name? I'm all the evil in the world, aren't I? All the betrayal, the broken hopes, the murderous revenge?

Maggie   And how'd that happen? Takes two to tango, kid.

With a sneer she opens the bottle. He stands at once.

Quentin   I'm not sitting here if you take any more. Especially on top of whiskey; that's the way it happened the last time.

She spills out a few into her palm and he walks a step away.

Okay. Carrie's in her room; I've told her to look in here every few minutes, and if she sees the signs she's to call the ambulance. Good night.

Maggie   She won't call the ambulance, she loves me.

Quentin   That's why she'll call the ambulance. Which is what I would have done last year if I'd loved you instead of loving myself. I'd have done it two years ago, in fact, but I didn't know what I know now.

Maggie (*sneering*)   What do you know now? You're spoiled. What do you know?

Quentin   A suicide kills two people, Maggie. That's what it's for. So I'm removing myself and perhaps it will lose its point.

She appears to consider for a moment; then carefully takes two pills and swallows them.

Right.

He walks, determined, upstage. And when he is a far distance:

Maggie (*on a new level; softly, and without any antagonism*)   What's Lazarus?

He halts, without turning back. She looks about for him, not knowing he has left.

Quentin?

Not seeing him, she starts up off the bed; a certain alarm . . .

Quen?

He comes halfway back.

Quentin   Jesus raised him from the dead. In the Bible. Go to sleep now.

Maggie   Wha's 'at suppose to prove?

Quentin   The power of faith.

Maggie   What about those who have no faith?

Quentin   They only have the will.

Maggie   But how you get the will?

Quentin   You have faith.

Maggie   Some apples.

He smiles, turns again to go.

I want more cream puffs.

He turns back; doesn't answer.

And my birthday dress? If I'm good? Mama? I want my mother.

She sits up, looks about as in a dream, turns and sees him.

Why you standing there?

She gets out of bed, squinting, and comes up to him, peers into his face; her expression comes alive.

You . . . you want music?

Quentin   All right, you lie down, and I'll put a little music on.

Maggie   No, you; you, sit down. And take off your shoes. I mean just to rest. You don't have to do anything. (*She goes to the machine, turns it on; jazz.*) Was I sleeping?

Quentin   For a moment, I think.

Maggie   Was she . . . was anybody else here?

Quentin   No. Just me.

Maggie   Is there smoke?

Quentin   Your mother's dead and gone, dear, she can't hurt you any more, don't be afraid.

Maggie (*in a helpless voice of a child*)   Where you going to put me?

Quentin (*his chest threatening a cry*)   Nowhere, dear – he'll decide with you. He might be here tonight.

Maggie   See? I'll lay down. (*She hurries to the bed, lies down.*) See?

Quentin   Good.

Maggie   'Member how used to talk to me till I went to sleep?

Quentin   Yes, dear. (*He sits beside the bed.*)

Maggie (*she struggles for lucidity, for some little pose of quiet charm*) It nice in Chicago?

Quentin   Yes, very nice. (*The caricature of the pleasantry nearly shakes off the world.*) Was it nice here?

Maggie (*she takes a strange, deep breath*)   Ya. Some birds came. And a mouse. You . . . you could have the pills if you want.

Quentin (*stands*)   I'll have Carrie come in and take them. (*He starts to move.*)

Maggie (*clutching the bottle*)   No. I won't give them to Carrie.

Quentin   Why do you want me to have them?

Maggie (*extending them*)   Here.

Quentin (*pause*)   Do you see it, Maggie? Right now? You're trying to make me the one who does it to you? I take them; and then we fight, and then I give them up, and you take the death from me. You see what's happening? You've been setting me up for a murder. Do you see it? (*He moves backward.*) But now I'm going away; so, you're not my victim any more. It's just you, and your hand.

Maggie (*slowly retracting her hand, looking at it*)   But ask Ludwig, I only wanted to be wonderful so you be proud, and you –

Quentin   And for yourself, dear, mostly for yourself. You were ambitious; it's no crime. You would have been everything you are without me.

Maggie (*about to weep*)   You ran out of patience, right?

Quentin   That's right. Yes.

Maggie   So you lied. Right?

Quentin   Yes, I lied. Every day. We are all separate people.

Maggie   You wanted a happy whore. Right?

Quentin   Not a whore, but happy, yes. I didn't want too much trouble.

Maggie   But Jesus must have loved her. Right?

Quentin   Who?

Maggie   Lazarus?

Quentin (*pause; he sees, he gropes toward his vision*)   That's right, yes! He loved her enough to raise her from the dead. But he's God, see –

Felice *appears, raising her arm in blessing.*

Quentin   . . . and God's power is love without limit. But when a man dares reach for that . . .

He has moved toward **Felice**, *pursuing his truth.*

Quentin   . . . he is only reaching for the power. Whoever goes to save another person with the lie of limitless love throws a shadow on the face of God. And God is what happened, God is what is; and whoever stands between another person and her truth is not a lover, he is . . .

He breaks off, lost, peering, and turns back to **Maggie** *for his clue, and as* **Felice** *vanishes . . .*

Quentin   And then she said.

He goes back to **Maggie**, *crying out to invoke her.*

Quentin   And then she said!

Maggie (*she is trying to wipe a film from before her thought*)   But . . . but . . . will my father find me if you put me . . . No. I mean – what's moral?

Quentin (*in the tension of trying to recall*)   To tell the truth.

Maggie   No – no . . . against yourself even.

Quentin   Yes.

Maggie (*she turns to him; her look is insane, and the truth is purified of all restraint*)   Well?

A cry is gathering in her, as though only now did she know there was no return.

I hear you. Way inside. Quentin? My love? I hear you! Tell me what happened!

Her tears tell her sanity. He weeps facing her.

Quentin (*on the verge of the abyss*)   Maggie, we . . . used one another.

Maggie (*weeping, calling*)   Not me, not me!

Quentin   Yes, you. And I. 'To live,' we cried, and 'Now,' we cried. And loved each other's innocence as though to love enough what was not there would cover up what was. But there is an angel, and night and day he brings back to us exactly what we want to lose. And no chemical can kill him, no blindness dark enough to make him lose his way; so you must love him, he keeps truth in the world. You eat those pills like power, but only what you've done will save you. If you could only say, I have been cruel, this frightening room would open! If you could say, I have been kicked around, but I have been just as inexcusably vicious to others; I have called my husband idiot in public, I have been utterly selfish despite my generosity, I have been hurt by a long line of men but I have cooperated with my persecutors . . .

Maggie (*she has been writhing, furious at this exorcism*)   Son of a bitch!

Quentin   And I am full of hatred, I, Maggie, the sweet lover of all life – I hate the world!

Maggie   Get out of here!

Quentin   Hate women, hate men, hate all who will not grovel at my feet proclaiming my limitless love for ever and ever!

She spills a handful of pills into her palm. He speaks desperately, trying not to physically take the pills from her.

Throw them in the sea; throw death in the sea and drink your life instead; your rotten, betrayed, hateful mockery of a life. That power is death, Maggie! Do the hardest thing of all – see our own hatred, and live!

Dumbly, she raises her hand toward her open mouth. He cannot hold back his hand and grips her wrist.

Maggie   What are you, goddamn judge or something? Let go. You no judge.

He lets go.

You know when I wanted to die. When I read what you wrote, judgey. Two months after we were married, judgey.

Quentin (*stricken, afraid, but remorseless*)   Let's keep it true. It's not some words on a piece of paper destroyed us. You told me you tried to die long before you met me.

Maggie   So you're not even there, huh. I didn't even meet you. (*Tries to laugh.*) You coward. Coward!

She staggers to her feet; he finds it hard to look directly at her. A clear line of accusation momentarily seems to steady her, and with the pills in her palm she stands straight.

I was married to a king, you son of a bitch! I was looking for a fountain pen to sign some autographs. And there's his desk . . .

She is speaking toward some invisible source of justice now, telling her injury.

. . . and there's his empty chair where he sits and thinks how to help people. And there's his handwriting. I wanted to touch his handwriting. And there's some words . . .

She almost literally reads in the air, and with the same original astonishment.

'The only one I will ever love is my daughter. If I could only find an honorable way to die.'

Now she turns to him.

When you gonna face that, judgey? Remember how I fell down fainted? On the new rug? 'Member? That's what killed me, judgey. Right?

She staggers up to him and into his face.

'Zat right? When you gonna face that one, kiddo?

Quentin (*a pause; he is struggling with her accusation and his guilt*) All right. You pour them back and I'll tell you the truth about that.

Maggie   You won't tell truth.

Quentin   I will now. (*He tries to tip her hand toward the bottle, holding both her wrists.*) You can hold the bottle, just pour them back.

Maggie (*closing her hand on the pills*)   But that's why, right?

Quentin (*with difficulty*)   We'll see. Pour them back, first.

She lets him pour them back, but she keeps the bottle. She sits staring on the bed, holding it in two hands.

Maggie (*she takes a deep breath*)   Liar.

Quentin (*in quiet tension against his own self-condemnation*)   We'd had our first party in our own house. Some important people, network heads, directors . . .

Maggie   And you were ashamed of me. Don't lie now! You're still playing God! That's what killed me, Quentin!

Quentin   All right. I wasn't . . . ashamed. But . . . afraid. (*Pause.*) I wasn't sure if any of them . . . had had you.

Maggie (*astounded*)   But I didn't know any of those!

Quentin (*not looking at her*)   I didn't know. But I swear to you, I did get to where none of it meant anything to me, I couldn't imagine what I'd ever been ashamed of. But it was too late. I had written that, and I was like all the others who'd betrayed you, and I could never be trusted again.

Maggie (*shaking her head; it is all corroborated*)   You never gave me a chance!

Quentin (*consumed, desperate for the slightest absolution*)   I did, Maggie, but it was too late. I laid down my life for you. But it was all too late.

Maggie (*with a mixture of accusation but near-sympathy*)   Why did you write that? (*She sobs, once.*)

Quentin   Because when the guests had gone, and you suddenly turned on me, calling me cold, remote, it was the first time I saw your eyes that way – betrayed, screaming that I'd made you feel you didn't exist.

Maggie   Don't mix me up with Louise!

Quentin   That's just it. That I could have brought two women so different to the same accusation – it closed a circle for me. And I wanted to face the worst thing I could imagine – that I could not love. And I wrote it down, like a letter . . . from myself.

She pours pills into her hand again.

I've told you the truth. That's rock bottom. What more do you want?

She starts to raise her hand to her mouth, and he steps in and holds her wrist.

What more do you *want*?

She looks at him, her eyes unreadable.

Maggie, we've got to have some humility toward ourselves; we were both born of many errors, a human being has to forgive himself! You want me to say I killed you? All right, I killed you. Now what? What do you want?

A strange calm overtakes her. She lies back on the bed. The hostility seems to have gone.

Maggie   Just . . . be human. And help me. And stop arguing.

He lets her hand go; it falls to the bed.

And love me. Sit on the bed.

He sits down.

Cover me.

He covers her.

And take down the sand dune. It's not too expensive. I wanted to hear the ocean when we made love in here but we could never hear the ocean.

Quentin   We're nearly broke, Maggie; and that dune keeps the roof from blowing off.

Maggie   Then you get a new roof. You'll have them take it away, right?

He doesn't answer.

I'm cold. Lie on me.

Quentin   I can't do that again, not when you're like this.

Maggie   Please. Just till I sleep!

Quentin (*breaking down*)   Maggie, it's a mockery. Leave me *something.*

Maggie   Just out of humanness! I'm cold!

Downing self-disgust, he lies down on her but holds his head away. Pause.

If you don't argue with me any more, I'll get rid of that other lawyer. 'Kay? If you don't argue? Ludwig doesn't argue.

He is silent.

And don't keep saying we're broke? And the sand dune?

The fear of his own total disintegration is growing in his face.

'Cause I love the ocean sound; like a big mother – sssh, sssh, sssh.

He slips off and stands looking down at her. Her eyes are closed.

You gonna be good now? 'Cause all I am . . . is love. And sex.

She takes a very deep, jagged breath.

Quentin *reaches in carefully and tries to slip the bottle out of her hand; she grips it.*

Maggie   Whyn't you lie on me?

Quentin (*as a fact, simply*)   It disgusts me.

Maggie   But if Lazarus . . .

Quentin   I am not the Savior and I am not the help . . . You are not going to kill me, Maggie, and that's all this is for!

Maggie   You liar!

Quentin   Not any more – I am not guilty for your life! I can't be. But I am responsible for it now. And I want those pills. I don't want to fight you, Maggie. Now put them in my hand.

She looks at him; then quickly tries to swallow her handful, but he knocks some of them out – although she swallows many. He grabs for the bottle but she holds and he pulls, yanks; she goes with the force and he drags her onto the floor, trying to pry her hands open as she flails at him and tears at his face, digs at his eyes. Her strength is wild and no longer her own, and, strangely, she is smiling, almost laughing. He grabs her wrist and squeezes it with both his fists.

Drop them, you bitch! You won't kill me!

She holds on, still smiling with a profound certainty, and suddenly, clearly, he lunges for her throat and lifts her with his grip.

You won't kill me! You won't kill me!

She drops the bottle as from the farthest distance **Mother** *rushes to a point crying out – the toy sailboat in her hand:*

Mother   Darling, open this door! I didn't trick you! I told Fanny to tell you we'd gone as soon you got up from your nap! I didn't trick you!

Quentin *springs away from* **Maggie**, *who falls back to the floor; his hands are open and in air.*

Mother   Quentin, why are you running water in there?

The sound of the sea comes up. **Mother** *backs away in horror.*

Stop that water! Quentin, I'll die if you do that! I saw a star when you were born, a light, a light in the world!

He stands transfixed as **Mother** *backs into his hand, and he begins to squeeze her throat and she to sink to the floor gasping for breath. He releases her in horror.*

Quentin   Murder?

Mother *stumbles into darkness, her hands in prayer, whispering, 'I will die, I will die.' He turns to* **Maggie**, *who is now getting to her hands and knees, gasping. He rushes to help her, terrified by his realization, but she flails out at him, and on one elbow looks up at him in a caricature of laughter, her eyes victorious and wild with fear.*

Maggie   Now we both know. You tried to kill me, mister. I been killed by a lot of people, some couldn't hardly spell, but it's the same, mister. You're on the end of a long, long line, Frank.

As though to ward off the accusation he desperately reaches again to help her up, and in absolute terror she skitters away across the floor.

Stay 'way! . . . No! N – no, Frank! Don't you do that!

Cautiously, as though facing a wild, ravening beast.

Don't you do that . . . or I call Quentin if you do that.

She glances off and calls quietly, but never leaving him out of her sight.

Quentin? Qu –?

She falls unconscious, crumpled on the floor, now with deep, strange breathing. He quickly goes to her, throws her over onto her stomach, starts artificial respiration, but just as he is about to start, he stands. He calls upstage.

Quentin　Carrie? Carrie!

Carrie *appears, praying, with open hands almost shielding her eyes. And, as though it were a final farewell –*

Quentin　Quick! Call the ambulance.

Carrie *bends to exorcise* **Maggie**'s *demons.*

Quentin　Stop wasting time! Call the ambulance!

Carrie *hurries out.*

Felice *appears; he hardly glances at her, comes down to the dock, halts.* **Felice** *remains behind him.*

Quentin　. . . No – no, we saved her. It was just in time. For her. But not for me. I knew why I had stayed; I packed up next morning. Her doctor tells me she had a few good months; he even thought for a while she was making it. Unless, God knows, he fell in love with her too.

He almost smiles; it is gone.

Look, I'll say it. It's really all I came to say. Barbiturates kill by suffocation. And the signal is a kind of sighing – the diaphragm is paralyzed.

With more difficulty.

And I'd noticed it when we'd begun to argue . . . I know, it usually does subside, but if not – each second can be most precious, why waste them arguing? What can be so important to gamble her life to get?

The tower lights, fierce, implacable.

. . . My innocence, you see? To get that back you kill most easily . . . No, don't; I want it . . . just the way it was.

He looks up.

And all those stars, still so fixed, so fortunate! And her precious seconds squirming in my hand like bugs; and I heard. Those deep, unnatural breaths, like the footfalls of my coming peace – and knew . . . I wanted them. How is that possible – I loved that girl!

Slight pause.

And the name . . . yes, the name . . .

Louise *appears, young, in her lab costume.*

Quentin   . . . in whose name do you ever turn your back . . .

He looks out at the audience.

. . . but in your own? In Quentin's name! Always in your own blood-covered name you turn your back!

Holga *appears on the highest level.*

Holga   But no one is innocent they did not kill!

Quentin   But love, is love enough? What love, what wave of pity will ever reach this knowledge – I know how to kill . . . I know, I know . . . she was doomed in any case, but will that cure? Or is it possible . . .

He turns toward the tower, moves toward it as toward a terrible God.

. . . that this is not bizarre . . . to anyone? And I am not alone, and no man lives who would not rather be the sole survivor of this place than all its finest victims? What is the cure? Who can be innocent again on this mountain of skulls? I tell you what

I know! My brothers died here . . . (*He looks down at the fallen* **Maggie**.) . . . but my brothers built this place; our hearts have cut these stones! And what's the cure!

Father *and* **Mother** *and* **Dan** *appear, and* **Lou** *and* **Mickey**; *all his people are in light now.*

Quentin   . . . No, not love; I loved them all, all! And gave them willingly to failure and to death that I might live, as they gave me and gave each other, with a word, a look, a truth, a lie – and all in love!

Holga   Hello!

Quentin   But what will defend her?

He cries up to her.

That woman hopes!

She stands unperturbed, resolute.

Or is that . . .

Struck – to the **Listener***:*

. . . exactly why she hopes, because she knows? What burning cities taught her and the death of love taught me – that we are very dangerous!

Staring, seeing his vision.

And that, that's why I wake each morning like a boy – even now, even now! I swear to you, there's something in me that could dare to love this world again! . . . Is the knowing all? To know, and even happily that we meet unblessed; not in some garden of wax fruit and painted trees, that lie of Eden, but after, after the Fall, after many, many deaths. Is the knowing all? And the wish to kill is never killed, but with some gift of courage one may look into its face when it appears, and with a stroke of love – as to an idiot in the house – forgive it; again and again . . . forever?

He is evidently interrupted by the **Listener**, *glances at his watch.*

. . . Yes, I don't want to be late. Thanks for making time for me . . . No, it's not certainty, I don't feel that. But it does seem feasible not to be afraid. Perhaps it's all one has. I'll tell her that . . . Yes, she will, she'll know what I mean. Well, see you again some time. Good luck, and thanks.

He turns upstage. He hesitates; all his people face him. He walks past **Louise***, pausing; but she turns her face away. He goes on and pauses beside* **Mother***, who lowers her head in uncomprehended sorrow, and gestures as though he touched her chin and she looks up at him and dares a smile, and he smiles back. He pauses at his dejected* **Father** *and* **Dan***, and with a look he magically makes them stand.* **Felice** *is about to raise her hand in blessing – he shakes her hand, aborting her enslavement.* **Mickey** *and* **Lou** *are standing together; he looks at them and neither of them are looking at him, but they move in behind him. Now he arrives at* **Maggie***; she rises from the floor webbed in with demons, trying to awake. And with his life following him he climbs toward* **Holga***, who raises her arm as though seeing him, and speaks with great love.*

Holga   Hello!

He comes to a halt a few yards from her. A whispering goes up from all his people. He straightens against it and walks toward her, holding out his hand.

Quentin   Hello.

The darkness takes them all.

Curtain.

Notes

3   *blasted stone tower of a German concentration camp*: the image
    of the guard tower, a visual representation of the
    Holocaust, is lit up at several points in the play when
    Quentin thinks of it.

3   *the Listener*: the character of the Listener never appears in
    the play but is to be seen as a constant offstage figure to
    whom Quentin is talking. In earlier drafts of the play,
    Miller identified this figure as a psychoanalyst whom
    Quentin hasn't seen in some time.

4   *Were you able to give me two hours?*: a surviving reference to
    the Listener's role as Quentin's psychoanalyist.

4   *I've quit the firm*: Quentin is a lawyer. This is a reference
    to his leaving his law firm, where he was a minor
    partner. In the final scene of the play (p. 128), he tells
    Maggie that he has just been fired from the firm for the
    second time.

5   *Columbia*: Columbia University in New York City.

7   *The Magic Flute*: *Die Zauberflöte* (1791), an opera by Wolfgang
    Amadeus Mozart (1756–91), who was born in Salzburg.

9   *She raises her arm in blessing*: Felice appears several times
    throughout the play making this gesture, which makes
    Quentin uncomfortable.

11 *Sylvia*: a reference to Quentin's sister, who does not
    appear in the play.

14 *two light fixtures*: Quentin makes several references to the
    fact that, if he stood between the light fixtures on the
    wall of his room, he would be in the posture of a
    crucified Christ (see p. 95).

15 *Spanish Republican Army*: during the Spanish Civil War
    (1936–9), Hitler supported the Fascist General Franco
    and the Nationalists against the left-wing Republicans.

15   *Strauss*: Johann Strauss II (1825–99) was the author of
      the waltz 'An der schönen blauen Donau' (1866), known
      in English as 'The Blue Danube'.

16   *forced labor for two years*: Holga, like her autobiographical
      model, Inge Morath, was forced to labour in a factory
      because she refused to join the Nazi youth organisation.

19   *Hiroshima*: the United States dropped an atomic bomb
      on Hiroshima in Japan on 6 August 1945, killing
      approximately 140,000 people and devastating the city.

21   *Fanny*: the maid.

22   *practice your penmanship*: Quentin's mother is very proud of
      her penmanship and her education in general. Quentin
      sees her efforts to get him to share her values as drawing
      him into being an 'accomplice' (p. 40) in what he sees as
      a betrayal of his father, for whose illiteracy she expresses
      contempt.

22   *Dempsey–Tunney fight*: this is probably a reference to the
      first meeting between the two heavyweight champions
      on 23 September 1926 in Philadelphia, when Gene
      Tunney beat the champion Jack Dempsey, becoming the
      new champion. The more famous fight between the two,
      the notorious 'long count' fight in Chicago in 1927, was
      also won by Tunney, after he had been knocked down
      earlier in the fight but, because of a delayed count by
      the referee, was able to get up and finish ten rounds,
      winning by unanimous decision.

23   *Vera Cruz, the Bismarck's due*: the Father's telephone calls
      indicate that he is in the shipping business, and is in
      crisis in the wake of the stock-market crash of 1929.
      Vera Cruz is a major port in Mexico. The *Bismarck*
      would be a ship in which Quentin's father has an interest
      (not the famous German battleship, which was not
      commissioned until the Second World War).

23   *ATO*: in another reference to shipping, ATO is a tariff
      code meaning 'assemble to order'.

23   *for once somebody was not going to break my mother's heart*:
      during the ellipsis, Quentin appears to have asked why
      his mother agreed to an arranged marriage with his
      father.

23   *Rachmaninoff*: Sergei Rachmaninoff (1873–1943), a well-known Russian composer.

24   *new Packard every year*: the Packard was a luxury automobile made by the American Packard Motor Car Company, later Studebaker-Packard, from 1899 to 1958. Buying three Packards for his relatives every year marks Quentin's father as both extravagant and generous.

24   *scholarship to Hunter*: Hunter College, now part of the City University of New York, was founded in 1870 as a Normal School or teacher-training school for young women. The fact that Quentin's mother was awarded a scholarship indicates that she was a promising student.

25   *get a shine*: a shoeshine; shoes were polished on the street by shoeshine boys.

27   *You are an idiot*: the Mother's insults to her husband's intelligence are repeated several times in the play, suggesting the lasting effect they had on Quentin and his feeling that they were a betrayal of his father. The word 'idiot' figures importantly, as Holga speaks of embracing her life as if it were an 'idiot child' (p. 28); Elsie calls Mickey a 'moral idiot' (p. 48); and, coming full circle, Quentin's wives use the word about him, as Louise says to him, 'Good God! What an idiot!' (p. 54) and Quentin complains about Maggie's calling him an idiot in public (p. 136).

28   *complicity*: an important theme in the play is Quentin's dawning awareness of a universal complicity in the evil that is done by one human being to another.

28   *I lost my memory*: the story that Holga tells reflects the wartime experience of Miller's third wife, Inge Morath.

29   *wurst*: sausage.

30   *It's Eden!*: Quentin refers nostalgically, if somewhat ironically, to a time 'before the Fall' when he believed in his own innocence and that of others. The naked figure of Elsie suggests Eve's temptation of Adam.

30   *refuses to wear silk stockings because the Japanese have invaded Manchuria*: Japan's invasion of Manchuria, a province of China, occurred in September 1931, after which Japan created a puppet state. To protest against this aggression,

some women in the US boycotted the silk that was
imported from the region.

32   *my being subpoenaed*: Lou refers to being called to testify in
front of the House Committee on Un-American
Activities.

32   *another attack might knock me off the faculty*: Lou teaches in a
law school. A number of academics who were called as
witnesses before the House Committee on Un-American
Activities lost their jobs, including faculty members at
the University of Michigan, Miller's alma mater.

33   *the day the world ended, it all fell down, and nobody was innocent
again*: this is Quentin's reference to the 'Fall' of the title,
the fall from grace, in the Christian interpretation, that
Adam and Eve experienced on behalf of the human
race; Miller focuses on the loss of innocence and the
knowledge of evil and guilt that followed.

35   *Betty*: Quentin and Louise's daughter.

41   *she's not your rib*: in the biblical story of Eden, Eve is made
from Adam's rib (Genesis 2:22).

42   *I'm . . . going to name names*: the witnesses who were called
before the House Committee on Un-American
Activities were subjected to a loyalty test of sorts by
being asked to name other people who had been
involved in activities with them, thus making them
vulnerable to being called to testify, blacklisted and
possibly jailed. 'Naming names' became a synonym for
informing and those who did it were shunned for
betraying their former comrades.

43   *this Fifth Amendment silence*: Americans are protected
against self-incrimination by the Fifth Amendment to
the Constitution; a number of witnesses who were called
before the House Committee on Un-American Activities
took refuge in the Fifth Amendment, refusing to answer
questions on the grounds that their answers might be
incriminating.

44   *As though – they would let me die*: this is a foreshadowing of
the worst thing that Quentin confesses about himself,
that he was willing to stand by and let Maggie die (pp.
142–3)

53   *I really don't want to be known as a Red lawyer*: in defending
      Lou, Quentin will be seen as someone who associates
      with Communists, and thus a 'Red' by association.

57   *You go back to work again tonight?*: Quentin is actually
      supposed to go back to work for a meeting about his
      defence of Lou, but he forgets or represses that fact.

58   *Perry Sullivan*: a fictional name, suggestive of the popular
      singer Perry Como and the well-known television
      personality Ed Sullivan.

60   *Park Avenue*: Park Avenue on the east side of Manhattan
      is one of the most exclusive and expensive streets in New
      York City and the last place Maggie might be expected
      to frequent.

60   *Judge Cruse*: because Quentin's law firm was closed for his
      funeral, Miller implies that Judge Cruse is a senior
      partner there.

64   *cruise in the forties*: Manhattan is laid out in a grid of
      numbered streets. Quentin is suggesting that Maggie go
      to the area around Times Square, where she might
      expect to find a record store.

78   *Idlewild*: John F. Kennedy Airport in New York was
      originally named Idlewild Airport after the golf course it
      displaced when it was constructed. It was renamed after
      Kennedy's assassination in 1963.

79   *Roosevelt*: Franklin D. Roosevelt (1882–1945), the thirty-
      second President of the United States and regarded by
      many as one of the greatest. He was first elected in 1932
      during the Great Depression and was responsible for the
      New Deal. He led the United States through most of the
      Second World War and was the only American president
      elected four times.

83   *there is never a depression for great people*: Quentin's mother is
      suggesting that his father would not have been ruined by
      the Great Depression if he had been 'great' himself.

83   *on the beach at Rockaway*: Rockaway Beach is on the south
      shore of Long Island in the New York borough of
      Queens. Like the Miller family, Quentin had a seaside
      vacation cottage.

84   *argyles*: socks with a diamond check, popular with golfers.

85   *Palladium*: the London Palladium is a West End theatre
     located off Oxford Street. During the 1920s, it was a
     vaudeville house. From 1955 to 1967, it was the venue
     for a variety show on ITV called *Sunday Night at the
     London Palladium*, which is presumably where Maggie is
     scheduled to appear.

85   *Ella Fitzgerald*: known as the 'first lady of song', Ella
     Fitzgerald (1917–96) was the most popular female jazz
     singer in the US during the mid-twentieth century.

86   *'Little Girl Blue'*: a song by Richard Rogers and Lorenz
     Hart, which first appeared in the musical *Jumbo* in 1935.
     It has been recorded by many popular and jazz singers.
     The best known renditions are by Nina Simone and
     Janis Joplin.

88   *El Morocco*: a New York supper club which was a
     favourite haunt of show-business celebrities during the
     1940s and 1950s.

89   *if I could see him*: the story that Maggie tells about her
     father echoes the real-life experience of Marilyn
     Monroe.

91   *Groton Shipyard*: Groton, Connecticut, is the location of
     the Electric Boat Corporation, which is the primary
     contractor for US Naval submarines and a major
     employer in eastern Connecticut.

95   *Gibson Girl*: the magazine illustrations of Charles Dana
     Gibson (1867–1944) featured a characteristic type that
     was known as the 'Gibson Girl'. She was tall, graceful
     and poised, wore her hair in a large chignon and often
     wore a big, plumed hat.

99   *Andy*: Maggie's agent, Andy, is based on Marilyn
     Monroe's business partner, Milton Greene, who engaged
     in similar shady dealings.

102 *French Provincial*: a style of furniture very popular in the
     US during the 1950s.

106 *First and Fifth Amendments to the Constitution*: the First
     Amendment to the Constitution of the United States
     protects freedom of speech, and the Fifth Amendment
     protects citizens against self-incrimination. Both were
     invoked by witnesses who were called before the House

Committee on Un-American Activities as protections
against being forced to answer questions.

109 *Ludwig Reiner*: Maggie's relationship with her singing
coach reflects Marilyn Monroe's relationship with Lee
Strasberg (1901–82), a well-known teacher at the Actors
Studio, where Monroe studied for a time, and purveyor
of the Method school of acting. Monroe's increasing
dependency on Strasberg and his wife Paula became a
strain on her marriage to Miller.

132 *Lazarus*: in the New Testament Bible (John 11), Jesus
brings Lazarus back to life after he has been entombed
for four days, a miracle which brought him many
followers.

141 *Frank*: Maggie seems to be hallucinating at this point, but
the name 'Frank' is probably an allusion to the popular
singer Frank Sinatra (1915–98), with whom Marilyn
Monroe had a romantic relationship after her divorce
from Miller in 1961.

144 *after the Fall*: Quentin's speech marks his rejection of 'that
lie of Eden' and the claim to innocence, and an
embracing of the knowledge that he is capable of evil
and that he must try to live his life with this knowledge.

Questions for Further Study

1 Choose one of the characters and explain how he or she is defined or limited by being filtered through Quentin's memory.

2 If you were directing the play, how would you direct the actors to approach the characters, given that they exist only in Quentin's memory?

3 Many reviewers of *After the Fall* have not understood the concept of the offstage Listener, thinking that Quentin was addressing the audience directly. Discuss Miller's use of the device in the play. How necessary is it to the reader/spectator's understanding?

4 Quentin describes himself as having a love–hate relationship with his mother. Does the character of the Mother as Miller develops her in the play justify Quentin's intense feelings about her? Do the episodes showing her betrayal of him and his father adequately explain his feelings?

5 Discuss the reasons for the failure of Quentin's marriage to Louise. Is Quentin right that she is at fault for refusing to say that any part of the failure was her responsibility?

6 Discuss the character of Mickey. Is he a representation of a 'moral idiot', as Elsie calls him, or is he more complex than that? Does his moral position have any validity?

7 Miller cut the character Felice when he adapted the play for television. Explain your agreement or disagreement with this move. Is Felice's significance clear in the play? Is she important to understanding Quentin and the play's meaning?

8 Quentin says that he and Maggie 'conspired to violate the past', denying some basic truths about themselves and their relationship, and so living in bad faith. Should the

failure of their marriage be ascribed to mutual bad faith? Is one of them more at fault than the other?

9 Quentin values Holga partly because she believes that no one can be sure they are living in good faith, which distinguishes her from Louise and Maggie, both of whom see themselves as innocent victims of the bad faith of others. In the context of the play, discuss your agreement or disagreement with Holga's statement.

10 There are several important religious references in *After the Fall*, most obviously to the Garden of Eden and Adam and Eve's fall from grace, but also to the crucifixion of Christ and the raising of Lazarus from the dead. Discuss the thematic effectiveness of these Christian allusions. Do they help Miller convey his ideas?

11 Miller's use of the Holocaust, both as a visual image, in the guard tower on the set and as a thematic representation for the evil that human beings were doing to each other in the twentieth century, has been controversial among critics of the play. Discuss the appropriateness and effectiveness of this element in the play.

12 Miller said that the philosophical basis of the play was suggested by Camus' novel *The Fall*, which he felt did not fully explore the implications of the basic issue of 'how one can ever judge another person once one has committed the iniquitous act of indifference to a stranger's call for help'. Discuss the effectiveness with which Miller develops this theme in *After the Fall*.

13 The issue of complicity is central to Miller's conception of guilt and responsibility in *After the Fall*. One of the play's most often-quoted lines is 'Who can be innocent again on this mountain of skulls?' Is the play convincing in its suggestion that we are all complicit in the human evil that is done in the world?

14 The thematic issue that frames Quentin's quest is the question of how to forgive oneself and live on once one recognises the evil that one is guilty of or capable of. Focusing particularly on the final scene with Maggie, discuss the effectiveness with which the play answers this question.

15 Many early critics saw Quentin, and by extension, Miller, as trying to justify himself in the play, an idea that Miller tried to refute. Is this point of view of the play justified?

16 What are the moral issues surrounding the House Committee on Un-American Activities that Miller suggests through the relationships among Lou, Mickey, Quentin and Elsie? Does he frame them in a convincing way?

17 Analyse Mickey's speech justifying his decision to name names. Are his arguments compelling? In the context of the play, would you direct the actor who plays Mickey to see this speech as a rationalisation or as a sincere explanation for his behaviour?

18 In his production, Michael Blakemore deliberately severed *After the Fall* from its autobiographical roots, particularly with regard to Maggie's character. Discuss the advantages and/or disadvantages of this approach.

19 The critic Michael Billington criticised *After the Fall* for failing to establish the logical connection between 'the individual capacity for murder and our assumed complicity in genocide'. Is this an appropriate criticism of the play?

20 Do you think Miller trivialises the Holocaust by using it as a framework in which to study the personal crisis of his central character?

21 Is it inevitable that *After the Fall* should be more powerful and effective on stage than on screen? How would you set about making a screen version?

BRENDA MURPHY is Board of Trustees Distinguished Professor of English at the University of Connecticut. Her many publications include *Congressional Theatre: Dramatizing McCarthyism on Stage, Film, and Television* (1999), *Miller: 'Death of a Salesman'* (1995), *The Provincetown Players and the Culture of Modernity* (2005), *O'Neill: 'Long Day's Journey Into Night'* (2001), *Tennessee Williams and Elia Kazan: A Collaboration in the Theatre* (1992), *American Realism and American Drama, 1880–1940* (1987) and, as editor, *Twentieth-Century American Drama: Critical Concepts in Literary and Cultural Studies* (2006), the *Cambridge Companion to American Women Playwrights* (1999), *Critical Insights: 'A Streetcar Named Desire'* (2010) and *Critical Insights: 'Death of a Salesman'* (2010). She has served as President of the American Theatre and Drama Society and the Eugene O'Neill Society, as well as on the board of the Arthur Miller Society.

ENOCH BRATER is the Kenneth T. Rowe Collegiate Professor of Dramatic Literature at the University of Michigan. He has published widely in the field of modern drama, and is an internationally renowned expert on such figures as Samuel Beckett and Arthur Miller. His recent books include *Arthur Miller: A Playwright's Life and Works, Arthur Miller's America: Theater and Culture in a Time of Change* and *Arthur Miller's Global Theater: How an American Playwright Is Performed on Stages around the World*.

Titles by Arthur Miller available from Methuen Drama

Scholarly Editions

Series Editor: Enoch Brater

After the Fall
edited by Brenda Murphy
ISBN 978 1 408 12312 6

All My Sons
edited by Toby Zinman
ISBN 978 1 408 10838 3

Broken Glass
edited by Alan Ackerman
ISBN 978 1 408 12884 8

The Crucible
edited by Susan C. W. Abbotson
ISBN 978 1 408 10839 0

The Last Yankee
edited by Katherine Egerton
ISBN 978 1 408 12315 7

The Price
edited by Jane K. Dominik
ISBN 978 1 408 12311 9

Death of a Salesman
edited by Enoch Brater
ISBN 978 1 408 108413

A Memory of Two Mondays
edited by Joshua Polster
ISBN 978 1 408 12316 4

A View from the Bridge
edited by Stephen Marino
ISBN 978 1 408 10840 6